Augsburg College
George Sverdrup Library
Minneapolis, MN 55454

D1171563

THE USE OF RESEARCH
IN SOCIAL WORK PRACTICE

THE USE OF RESEARCH IN SOCIAL WORK PRACTICE_____

A Case Example
from School Social Work

Nancy Feyl Chavkin

Augsburg College
George Sverdrup Library
Minneapolis, MN 55454

Westport, Connecticut
London

Library of Congress Cataloging-in-Publication Data

Chavkin, Nancy Feyl.
    The use of research in social work practice : a case example from
school social work / Nancy Feyl Chavkin.
        p   cm.
    Includes bibliographical references and index.
    ISBN 0–275–94648–7 (alk. paper)
        1. Social service—Research—United States.   2. School social
work–United States–Case studies.   I. Title.
HV11.C485   1994
371.4'6—dc20   93–19111

British Library Cataloguing in Publication Data is available.

Copyright © 1993 by Nancy Feyl Chavkin

All rights reserved. No portion of this book may be
reproduced, by any process or technique, without the
express written consent of the publisher.

Library of Congress Catalog Card Number: 93–19111
ISBN: 0–275–94648–7

First published in 1993

Praeger Publishers, 88 Post Road West, Westport, CT 06881
An imprint of Greenwood Publishing Group, Inc.

Printed in the United States of America

The paper used in this book complies with the
Permanent Paper Standard issued by the National
Information Standards Organization (Z39.48–1984).

10 9 8 7 6 5 4 3 2 1

Copyright Acknowledgments

Material in Appendix B originally published as Costin, L. B. (1969a). An analysis of the tasks in
school social work. *Social Service Review, 43*, 274–285. Reprinted with permission of the
University of Chicago Press. Copyright 1969 by the University of Chicago.

Tables 3.1 and 3.2 are reprinted from "An Axiomatic Theory of Organizations" by Jerald Hage,
published in *Administrative Science Quarterly*, 10, no. 3 (December 1965) by permission of
Administrative Science Quarterly. Copyright 1965 by the Graduate School of Business and Public
Administration.

V
485
993

Dedicated in honor of
Marie Feyl
Sylvia Chavkin
and Gilbert Chavkin;
and in memory of Sam Feyl

Contents

Tables and Figures

TABLES

FIGURES

Preface

This book would not have been possible without the support of others. It is my pleasure to express thanks to Prof. David Austin of the University of Texas at Austin and to Prof. Lela Costin of the University of Illinois.

I also benefited from the support of Karen Brown of the Walter Richter Institute of Social Work, Paul Kennedy of the Partnership for Access To Higher Mathematics Program, and Marion Tangum of the Office of Sponsored Programs. Tina Jackson, Anne Byrd, and Susan Bergfield helped prepare the final tables and illustrations for the manuscript, and a number of Southwest Texas State University student assistants helped with the word processing.

My greatest debt is to my husband, Allan Chavkin, for his insightful comments and constructive criticism throughout the project and to our daughter, Laura Chavkin, for her patience and enthusiastic support.

PART I

SOCIAL SCIENCE RESEARCH
AND SOCIAL WORK PRACTICE

1 Social Work's Relationship to Social Science Research

The Task Force on Social Work Research (1991) begins its report by discussing the nature and causes of the crisis in social work research. Social work practice depends upon research in order to find the most effective ways to deal with social problems. Fanshel (1980) has aptly pointed out that research is essential for two key reasons—the profession's self-respect and the positive regard of outsiders. The National Institute of Mental Health (1991) makes an even stronger statement about the importance of social work research as it describes the work domain of social work as touching on a multitude of human problems that inflict pain and suffering on millions of individuals and families.

HISTORICAL BACKGROUND

Since the creation of the American Social Science Association in 1865, the field of sociology and the crusade for social reform have always been closely linked. Anthony Oberschall's historical account (1973) of the purpose of the American Social Science Association stresses its twofold nature to aid in the development of social science and to guide the public about practical affairs. Social work has been actively involved in the application of rational science to the social problems of the time. The first meeting of the National Conference of Charities and Corrections, the predecessor of National Conference on Social Welfare, was hosted by the American Social Science Association in 1874 (Zimbalist 1977).

Similar accounts of this close relationship between social science and social reform are offered by Pauline Young in her 1946 review of the social survey movement and by Luther and Jessie Bernard in their work, *The Origins of American Sociology* (1943). In addition, Paul Lazarsfield and Jeffrey Reitz describe early college sociology courses "as likely to be taught by Protestant ministers interested in various reform movements" (1975, p. 1). Young and the

Bernards support their argument with a quotation from the catalog of the first graduate department of sociology at Columbia University in 1894, which states that New York City "is a natural laboratory of social science."

Although the relationship between sociology and the crusade for social reform is well established, the subject is a complex one. Lazarsfield and Reitz (1975) have developed a schema that presents the historical evolution of the issues involved. Phase 1 is described as the period where the need for social improvement and the work of the sociologist was not distinguished. Phase 2 was the time when there were efforts to establish sociology as a field of knowledge independent of any concrete social goal. Phase 3 is the current search for a new synthesis between sociological knowledge and practical work.

This book's case example from school social work falls within phase 3 because it is an attempt to understand factors affecting the utilization of a recommendation from social science research in the practical world.

DEFINITIONS

A problem with terminology immediately surfaces with the phrase "social science research." A distinction is often made between two kinds of social science research—basic and applied. Despite the sometimes confusing distinction between basic and applied research, the work of Cherns (1970) is well accepted and is employed in the present study. Cherns divides social science research into four categories (two basic and two applied):

1. *Pure basic research* is research arising out of perceived needs of the discipline and is, generally speaking, oriented toward resolving or illuminating or exemplifying a theoretical problem.

2. *Basic objective research* is oriented toward a problem that arises in some field of application of the discipline, but is not aimed at prescribing a solution to a practical problem.

3. *Operational research* is aimed at tackling an ongoing problem within some organizational framework but does not include or involve experimental action. This kind of research is distinguished by its strategy and methods. Broadly speaking these are: (a) observation of the "mission" of the organization; (b) identification of its goals; (c) establishment of criteria of goal attainment; (d) devising measures for assessing performance against these criteria; (e) carrying out these measurements and comparing them with the goals; (f) completing the feedback loop by reporting on the discrepancy between goal and achievement. In the course of an operational research, project changes may occur as a result of the inquiries of the operational researchers, but this is not perceived as the aim of the research, although it may be a more-or-less welcome concomitant of it.

4. *Action research* may involve as part of its strategy a piece of operational research but is distinguished from an ordinary piece of operational research by the addition to the strategy of the introduction and observation of planned change. The change proposed

may be arrived at as a result of a piece of operational research and operational research techniques are often used within a scheme of action research (Cherns 1970, p. 235).

The school social work example in this book fits between Chern's third and fourth definition of operational research because it is aimed at tackling an ongoing problem within some organizational framework and also proposes a change. Pure operational research means the results are in the form of data and facts and do not include recommendations. There are also proposals for innovation based on research where the researcher has utilized personal values and knowledge of the world in combination with research findings. The current study examines a proposal for innovation because it looks at the utilization of Lela Costin's (1969a) recommendation for a changed goal for school social work. Costin combined her research findings, her interpretation of history, her personal values, and her experiences in making her recommendation for change.

THE ISSUE OF RESEARCH UTILIZATION

The examination of the association between organizational structure and the utilization of Costin's recommendation is part of a much larger issue in applied social science research. Social science and its relationship to the practical world has always been a complex subject, and the present study addresses the problem of what factors affect the utilization of applied social science research by using organizational theory to examine the use of a specific research recommendation in the field of school social work.

There is no doubt that social science research is of critical importance to social work practice (Briar, Weissman, & Rubin 1981, Rosenblatt 1968, LeCroy, Ashford, & Macht 1989, Task Force on Social Work Research 1991, Videka-Sherman 1986), but many questions still remain about what factors influence social workers' use of research findings. The National Institute of Mental Health (1991) says that in addition to more research we need to improve the usefulness of research. As Reid (1993) states, "the bottom line of a profession's research activity is found in what happens to the products of this activity."

Two major conferences (the Conference on Research Utilization in Social Work, sponsored by the Social Work Training Branch of the National Institute of National Health in 1976, and the Conference on Research and Information Utilization in Social Work, sponsored by Boysville Institute and Wayne State University School of Social Work in 1989) both highlighted the need to know more about research utilization. The first conference laid the groundwork for stimulating the social work profession to identify ways to improve research utilization and to encourage the teaching of research. The second conference built upon the work of the first conference and extended it by considering the past experiences of researchers and educators in the decade that had passed, by addressing the issue of research utilization in agencies, and by looking at the role of computers in the research utilization process (Grasso & Epstein 1992).

Researchers first approached the utilization issue from the perspective that researchers were not producing usable, timely, and appropriate information for practice (Patton 1979, Weiss 1977, Weiss & Bucuvalas 1980). Dery (1986) proposed that the second stage of the utilization issue was an acknowledgment that government agencies (and social work organizations in the same line of reasoning) don't really use research. At a March 1991 conference in New York City (Mattaini 1992) the idea was presented that practice and research in social work should be intertwined and not integrated. The premise was that research utilization would increase with close collaboration rather than integration of the two fields.

The whole concept of use has become ambiguous, and researchers have focused their attention on individual users and the differences between research and practice. Primarily researchers have looked at individual thoughts, perceptions, values, ways of operating (Beyer & Trice 1982, Caplan 1976, Dery 1986, Patton 1979). It is important for social work research to now shift the focus from the individual to the organization as the unit of analysis.

Organizations are complex, and we do not know enough about how they use research. Weissman (1992) concurs that researchers need to understand how the knowledge and information they generate is used by policymakers and administrators. Mizrahi (1992) suggests that supply and demand issues affect the utilization of research in community practice settings. Hasenfeld and Patti (1992) are quite confident about the possibility of ever reconciling the needs of organizational administrators and research; they propose ''reflection-in-action'' as the appropriate model for research utilization. Acknowledging that research utilization is not always a rational process, they too suggest we need to understand more about the organizational context of research utilization.

PURPOSE OF CASE STUDY

The major purpose of the case study reported in Part II is to test the theory that there is a relationship between organizational structure and the utilization of a research recommendation. It is based on the need for school social workers to understand more about organizational structure factors that may facilitate or inhibit their adoption of Costin's recommendation for a change in social service delivery methods. No attempt is made through the study to promote or retard the utilization of the research recommendation; the intent of the study is empirical. In addition, it is not assumed that more or less use of a research recommendation is necessarily better or worse; the key goal is to understand the organizational structure factors that have resulted in the utilization/nonutilization of Costin's recommendation.

SIGNIFICANCE OF STUDY

The significance of the study is embellished if one looks at the rise in both number and cost of social science research studies. The National Academy of

Science (1978) reports that $1.2 billion was spent in 1976 for knowledge production, and this amount has only grown higher, with the increased evaluation provisions to Congressional program funding (Weiss & Bucuvalas 1980). Similar accounts of this burgeoning interest in public policy as the object of scientific study are presented by Mayer and Greenwood (1980) in their account of the variety of applied research projects being funded in an attempt to utilize systematic planning and management for social and environmental problems. The rationale for spending public monies on research studies has frequently been their assumed usefulness in improving programs and developing policies (Weiss 1972); however, these claims are countered by widespread reports on nonutilization of results (Cook 1978, Weiss & Bucuvalas 1980). Lawrence Lynn's book *Knowledge and Policy: The Uncertain Connection* (1978) underscores this loss of faith in the utilization of research, and thus it is imperative that the factors that affect utilization of research be examined.

Further, the results of the current study may be significant in enhancing recent attempts by social workers to understand the research-policy linkage. Rothman (1980) tries to build a bridge between social science research and human service practice by concentrating on the practical. He conceptualizes the utilization process that takes place in translating a research finding to an application concept that can possibly guide practice. He identifies two steps of conversion (formulation of a basic prescription from the research) and design (procedures for implementing the prescription). In addition, Tripodi, Fellin, and Meyer (1969) suggest individual guidelines for the utilization of research. Also, Mullen (1978) utilizes a systems framework to structure the utilization process and then describes how to construct personal working models for research utilization.

Despite the increased attention being paid to research utilization by social workers and the acknowledgment of the complexity of the issues, a significant gap exists in the conceptualization of research utilization. Rothman (1980) focuses on the role of the individual in his guidelines for conversion and design. Tripodi, Fellin, and Meyer's suggestions (1969) and Mullen's personal working models (1978) also concern the individual social worker. Zimbalist (1977) in his historical overview discusses political, economic, and social factors which influence research utilization. Individual and extraorganizational perspectives on research utilization have been presented, but little consideration has been given to an organizational perspective.

The organizational perspective is an important one for social work because social work is an organizationally based profession. Social workers are highly influenced by the organizations in which they work and cannot be considered primarily a profession of individual, private practitioners. An overwhelming number of social workers, like human service workers in general, spend their entire careers working in one organization or another. The organization shares the "needs" and the "problems": it selects the techniques utilized to deal with problems. According to Zald (1967), the fates of clients and the methods of service delivery are profoundly affected by the organizational context, and this is why it is essential to know more about how the school as an organization impacts on the school social worker's utilization of a research recommendation.

Williams (1970) points out that less effective professional service results when school social workers are employed in incompatible school situations. For example, it matters what the relationship is between the social worker and principal in the school. Rowen (1965), Fisher (1966), and Flynn (1976) discuss the problems of role incongruence between the school social worker and other organizational members.

Constable (1979) suggests that if school social workers do not define their role, they will have it defined for them. The question of role and professional autonomy is highly influenced by the organizations in which school social workers are employed; Steiner (1979) discusses how inadequately prepared school social workers are for dealing with the organizations in which they work.

Brown (1982) highlights the need for the school social worker to be knowledgeable about the school as an organization because the school impacts so strongly upon the role of the school social worker. Brown suggests that using the school as a unit of analysis can expand the view of school social workers as they try to locate the reasons for the problems they are trying to solve. The school is very definitely an organization; it is a social system directed toward achieving the goal of education. The school is a human service organization according to Hasenfeld and English (1974), a socialization agency according to Vinter (1963), and a service organization according to Blau and Scott (1962).

It is important to conceptualize the school as an organization and to understand that school social workers perform their roles within this organization. Organizational analysis should be part of more studies of school social work. The study is an attempt to understand more about one part of the organization, organizational structure and the utilization of Costin's recommendation (1969a).

ORGANIZATION OF BOOK

For the first time, this book examines the influence of organizational structure on the use of a specific research finding in school social work. This organizational perspective will add to the paucity of information social workers have about why research findings are adopted in some organizations and not in others.

The book is organized into three parts. Part I contains three chapters that explore the complex relationship between applied social science research and practice. Part II is a case example where I examine the use of a specific research recommendation in the field of school social work. Part III presents the results and implications of the case study for practice, policy, and theory, and it provides suggestions for future research.

In Part I, Chapter 1 poses the problem and its significance for social work. Chapter 2 analyzes previous work on research use and innovation and presents the current concerns. Chapter 3 provides the theoretical context of this study, an organizational perspective utilizing the theory of Hage and Aiken (1970).

In Part II, Chapter 4 discusses the historical background of Costin's recommendation for a change in the goal and activities of school social work, the research finding being studied. Chapter 5 describes the methodology including theoretical assumptions, hypotheses, variables and their measurement, population and sample, instruments, and procedures for data collection and analysis. Chapter 6 presents the characteristics of the sample studied.

In Part III, Chapter 7 contains the results of the analysis of the data and the examination of the central problem of the case study—the utilization of Costin's research recommendation. Chapter 8 addresses the practice, policy, and theoretical implications of the study, and it discusses recommendations for future research.

2 Previous Studies on Research Utilization and Innovation

The investigation of why Costin's recommendation (1969a) for a change in social service delivery methods was utilized in some school districts, adapted in others, and rejected in still others involved a study of the adoption of a particular type of innovation, an innovation based on the utilization of a research recommendation. For this reason, it is necessary to review two fields of literature—research utilization and innovation. After a review of the major ideas and research, the current concerns of this study will be presented. The discussion includes how the present investigation furthers the study of both research utilization and innovation.

RESEARCH UTILIZATION STUDIES

Studies in the field of research utilization have been quite recent, and there are five major studies (Weiss & Bucuvalas 1980, Alkin et al. 1979, Caplan et al. 1975, Patton et al. 1977, Rich 1977) which are critical to the understanding of both the very broad topic of research utilization and the more specific issue of utilization of a research recommendation. These five studies will be reviewed, and then several important issues relating to theory, definitions of utilization, methodology, and variables studied will be addressed in relation to studying the utilization of Costin's recommendation.

Weiss and Bucuvalas

Weiss and Bucuvalas (1980) interviewed 255 people (155 decision makers in mental health agencies, 50 members of mental health research review committees, and 50 social scientists who had conducted mental health research) in order to understand decision makers' responses to research studies on topics relevant to their work, particularly the conditions under which they found research useful,

Augsburg College Library

and if, when, and how they applied the research to the work they did. The interviews consisted of the respondents' reading and rating of abstracts of actual research reports of studies that had been funded by federal mental health bodies. Each report was rated on several measures of usefulness and on twenty-nine descriptive characteristics. Weiss and Bucuvalas hypothesized that decision makers' ratings of specific studies would yield three sets of factors—implementability, scientific merit, and political acceptability.

The results were that five characteristics of research studies affect utilization—relevance, research quality, conformity with user expectations, action orientation, and challenge to status quo. All were positively correlated with utilization. The researchers divided these characteristics into a truth test (research quality and conformity with user expectations) and a utility test (action orientation and challenge to status quo), which are conducted after the research is deemed relevant. The one unexpected finding was challenge to status quo. The researchers had hypothesized that this would be negatively related to utilization, but instead they found it was positively related. Weiss and Bucuvalas account for this unexpected result by suggesting that challenge to the status quo means research is used to stimulate thought and provide divergent perspectives that may not be immediately used but will perhaps be used in future decisions.

This study added important large-scale quantitative data on research characteristics that influence the decision to use a research report's recommendation. It also employed a broad definition of utilization, which measured usefulness on a scale of 1 to 5 in four areas (likelihood of own use, substantive usefulness in own agency, likelihood of use by most appropriate user, and substantive usefulness by most appropriate agency). The weaknesses of the study are that it focused only on the outcome of the research utilization process, the decision, and it used hypothetical examples. Weiss and Bucuvalas recommend that future research needs to examine fields other than mental health and to study the conditions and processes of actual research utilization.

Alkin et al.

The qualitative study by Alkin et al. (1979) explored the impact of evaluations on five school systems. It specifically sought to find the factors that influenced the decision to utilize or not utilize the evaluation findings. The schools had all recently completed a Title I or Title III project evaluation and were receptive to the study. A broad definition of utilization was used, what the authors term an "alternative definition." Utilization included long range and subtle effects of the evaluation as well as specific decisions, and process as well as outcome was examined. No specific hypotheses were proposed, and both open- and close-ended questions were used in the interview.

The study yielded an analytic framework consisting of eight categories of variables that affect the decision to utilize evaluation findings: preexisting evaluation conditions, orientation of the users, evaluator's approach, evaluator credibility, organizational factors, extraorganizational factors, information content and reporting, and administrator style. It is an important utilization study because it attempts to examine the course, role, and consequences of evaluation and is much more comprehensive than most studies.

The major limitation of the research is its generalizability because of the way the cases were selected. Approachability, proximity, prior knowledge of, and suggestions from colleagues were listed as considerations in selecting the five sites. Recommendations for the future are to identify formally all eight categories of variables affecting utilization. The current study attempts to understand more about Alkin's category of organizational factors.

Caplan et al.

Caplan and his associates (1975) conducted 204 interviews on social science research utilization in an attempt to explore the use of social science knowledge in policy-related decision-making among upper level officials in the executive branch of the United States government. The questions were in six general categories: (1) respondent's awareness of available, relevant social science information, knowledge and use of sources, and information retrieval practices; (2) respondent's self-reported use of social science knowledge in policy relevant situations; (3) respondent's interest in the development of social indicators; (4) respondent's evaluation of worth and perceived objectivity of various kinds of social science data, data collection methods, and degree of confidence in various disciplines; (5) respondent's attitudes and beliefs about social science research and utilization; and (6) respondent's personal and educational background, employment, and career plan.

Three general theories of nonutilization formed the framework of the questions; no specific hypotheses were presented. The theories were knowledge-specific theories, two-communities theories, and policymaker-constraint theories. The knowledge-specific theories attempt to explain the decision not to use social science knowledge by looking at the inadequacies of the social science knowledge—i.e., its overreliance on quantitative methods, methodological inadequacies, its impracticality, its lack of action, its political overtones. The two-communities theories attempt to explain the decision not to utilize information in terms of the differences between producer and user. Policymaker-constraint theories look at the problems and multiple variables involved in utilizing information as the reason for the decision not to utilize knowledge.

The results were that social science research was used with a modest level of satisfaction; however, hard data were minimally used and "soft" data had widespread use. Factors affecting utilization were attitudes toward social science research, political factors, and user style. User style was divided into three categories: (1) clinical; (2) academic; and (3) advocacy. Clinical respondents looked at research from both an internal logic perspective (scientific accuracy) and an external logic perspective (value-based, political, economic, and administrative components of the problem). Clinical respondents reported the highest degree of use. Academic users (internal logic) were the next highest users and advocacy users (external logic) were the least users of social science research.

The strengths of Caplan and his associates' study lie in its comprehensive interviews of over 200 executive level decision makers. It is an excellent exploratory study, and future needs of more quantitative studies, more longitudinal studies, and more cross-national studies are pointed out by the researchers.

Patton et al.

The purpose of Patton et al.'s research (1977) was to assess the degree to which evaluations were used and to identify and refine a few key variables that might be important for the utilization of evaluations. The stratified random sample consisted of twenty case studies of federal health evaluations that had recently been completed. The key informants were project officers, decision makers, and evaluators. Open-ended interviews were conducted with each of these persons.

The findings indicated that evaluation did have an impact on program, but the typical impact was generally not very clear or dramatic. Rather, impact was defined as "an additional input into an ongoing, evolutionary process of program action." Individual decision makers used evaluation research most often in order to reduce their uncertainty in dealing with complex programming. Evaluations were viewed as one piece of data in the decision-making process.

Two major factors affecting utilization were a political factor and a "personal factor." The political factor was an expected result since the political nature of evaluation research has been well-documented, but the personal factor was not expected. The personal factor consisted of leadership, interest, enthusiasm, determination, commitment, aggressiveness, and caring. This factor emerged when respondents were asked which of eleven factors was most important in explaining the impact or nonimpact of an evaluation. The responses were always in terms of individuals, not in terms of factors.

The study by Patton and his associates offers much to the field of research utilization studies, because it used actual studies, a broad definition of utilization, and interviewed a more representative sample than previous studies. Its weaknesses are that it is a retrospective study looking at what respondents recall about the evaluations and that it is primarily outcome oriented. Its major future recommendations include further study of both political and personal factors.

Rich

Rich's study (1977) used the experiences of the Continuous National Survey with clients in seven federal domestic service-oriented agencies to examine the question "how is public opinion data used by policymakers in making decisions?" During an eighteen month period in which the Continuous National Survey was used, thirty-eight respondents were interviewed on five different occasions and then they were interviewed nine months later. Documentation (in the form of memos, letters, telephone logs) was also collected.

Utilization of information was broken down into two categories—instrumental and conceptual. Instrumental use referred to cases where respondents cited and could document actual use for decision making. Conceptual use referred to influencing a policymaker's thinking about an issue or to planned future use of the information.

The results suggested that two cycles of utilization were associated with the agency's processing of data from the Continuous National Survey. The first wave or short-term utilization was primarily for instrumental purposes and usually occurred within three months. The flow of information was primarily upward through the decision-making hierarchy.

The research was originally based on the hypothesis that the two-communities theory would be evident, but the findings did not suggest that these assumptions were completely valid. In contrast to the hypothesis, policymakers valued research results and were receptive to developing new information capacities. Also the policymakers interviewed were knowledgeable about research methods and the needs/constraints affecting the research community. The lack of support for the two-communities theory is explained by the use of both conceptual and instrumental definitions of use. It is suggested that further research be done using a broad definition of use.

The strengths of this study are its present focus and its ability to monitor an ongoing decision process over an eighteen-month period. Its weaknesses are that its sample may not be representative and it does focus primarily on outcome.

Rich's recommendations for future study are critical. He calls for further examination of conceptual use, which is still vaguely described in the literature. He suggests a need to look more at evaluation and research as it is occurring, i.e., continuous studies so that process and longitudinal data can be examined.

Definition of Utilization

The definition of utilization is a critical factor in any analysis of research utilization. When utilization was defined narrowly (instrumental or documented use only), as in the case of Knorr (1977), little use could be found. It was not until the definition was extended to include items which are often categorized as conceptual use (influenced thinking) that Knorr was able to find evidence of research utilization. Caplan et al. (1975), Patton et al. (1977), Rich (1977), and Alkin et al. (1979), all looked for broad possibilities of use and concluded that more attention needs to be paid to conceptual use, soft data, attitudes, long-range use, and subtle effects. Weiss and Bucuvalas (1980) were the first to use a rating scale for instrumental and conceptual use, and this scale has added an important new dimension to the definition of utilization. A similar rating scale will be employed in the present inquiry for instrumental and conceptual use.

Theoretical Perspectives

The most frequently cited theoretical base for most of the studies on research utilization has been decision-making theory. The research projects assume that the decision-making process is a cycle of events (Litchfield, 1956) that includes several steps—the identification of a problem, the development of a plan to alleviate the problem, the initiation of the plan, and the evaluation of its success or failure. Caplan et al. (1975), Pattan et al. (1977), Rich (1977), Alkin et al. (1979), and Weiss and Bucuvalas (1980) all follow this tradition.

Some of the empirical studies (Brown et al. 1978, Thompson et al. 1981, and Williams & Wysong, 1977) use communication theory in combination with decision-making theory. Brown et al. (1978) found that their hypothesis (the manner in which results were reported would directly affect the decision) was unsubstantiated, but Thompson et al. (1981) found that the characteristics of the audience (to whom results were reported) did have a significant impact on the decision. Williams and Wysong (1980) reported that the structural relationships of an organization may affect how, when, and what data gets communicated, and thus these structural relationships might affect the decision-making process. Rich (1981) looked at the structure of the decision-making process and sought to discover if it follows a bureaucratic model or a modern policy analyst model. He found that a bureaucratic model was reported to the public, but in reality informal relations and informal communication (the modern policy analyst model) were major factors.

A few authors have referred to theories of organizational constraints (Kogan 1963, Rodney & Kolodney 1964, Patton et al. 1977, Alkin et al. 1979, Weiss 1981), but the theories have not been empirically tested. The Getzels-Guba model (1957) postulates that social behavior in a school is affected by institutional expectations, group intentions, and individual needs, but little work has been done on the relationship between institutional expectations and research utilization. Simon's (1976) work on the organization's need to "satisfice" (look for a "good enough" course of action) is frequently referenced, but no study on the utilization of research has actually examined organizational variables in any depth. Despite the fact that authors (Blau 1955, Griffiths 1964, Abbott 1965, Thompson 1965, Bennis 1971) have theorized that organizational structure affects the flow of knowledge into and within organizations, most research utilization studies only hint at a possible relationship between organizational theories and the use of research.

In short, a wide variety of research utilization studies exist, but no studies have employed theories of organizational structure as the conceptual basis of their research. In accord with the work of Hage and Aiken (1970) on the importance of the structural characteristics of formal organizations to the process of program change, this study uses organizational theory as its conceptual framework. Specifically it tests the theory that there is a relationship between organizational structure and the utilization of a research recommendation in school social work.

Methodology

Four of the major research utilization studies (Caplan et al. 1975, Patton et al. 1977, Rich 1977, Alkin et al. 1979) used qualitative methods to examine the factors which affect utilization by conducting a series of interviews. Alkin et al. (1979) used five case studies of educational evaluations and interviewed key persons in each; Patton et al. (1977) followed up twenty health evaluations and interviewed three key informants for each; Rich (1977) interviewed thirty-eight respondents to the Continuous National Survey on five occasions; and Caplan et al. (1975) interviewed 204 federal level officials. The major quantitative study was done by Weiss and Bucuvalas (1980), and it was an attempt to quantify the factors that affect decision makers' responses to research.

It is clear that the majority of past studies have relied very heavily on open-ended interviews and questionnaires with little information provided on reliability of judgments and few attempts at inter-rater reliability. Weiss and Bucuvalas's study (1980) is important because it provided an initial framework for specifying variables and used rating scales. According to these authors, future studies could be enhanced by concentrating on a representative sample of cases from one content area: focusing on organizations and not just decision makers, using present-time orientations, and conducting more quantitative studies.

Variables Studied

Many variables describing the research utilization process have been identified and studied. Weiss and Bucuvalas (1980) proposed five categories—relevance, research quality, conformity with user expectations, action orientation, and challenge to the status quo. Alkin et al. (1979) suggested preexisting evaluation bounds, user orientation, evaluator approach, evaluator credibility, organizational factors, information context and report, and administrator report. Thompson et al. (1981) looked at audience characteristics, Patton et al. (1977) examined political and personal factors, and Brown et al. (1978) focused on the report. Because a wide variety of variables have been considered, it is necessary to continue categorizing these variables and then delineating their subcomponents through empirical research.

In a review of research utilization literature by Levitan and Hughes (1981), five clusters of variables (relevance, communication, information processing, credibility, and user involvement/advocacy) were suggested. Conner's review (1981) of utilization studies categorized variables by looking at whether they are related to goals, inputs, processes, or outcomes. The suggestion for categorization in the current study differs from these reviews and from the research of

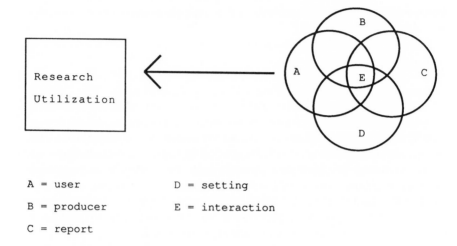

A = user   D = setting

B = producer   E = interaction

C = report

Figure 2.1 Variable Categorization

Alkin et al. (1979), Weiss and Bucuvalas (1980), and others because it is more comprehensive and more clearly represents the total utilization process. The categorization focuses on the principal actors (user and producer), the report (including data collection and dissemination), the setting (organizational factors, both internal and external), and the interaction among them. The categorization of variables is schematically shown in Figure 2.1 by four interlocking circles.

All of the variables previously identified by research and reviews of the literature can fit into this categorization, and all the variables have possible effects on the utilization process. The category of variables that has been given the least attention in the empirical research is the setting. This study's focus on internal organizational structure (part of the setting category) is looking at a small segment of the utilization process. The producer (Professor Costin) and the report (journal article/research) will be constant. It is assumed that opportunity for interaction between producer, user, setting, and report can also be held constant by sample selection (looking at school districts within states with state associations of school social work that provide similar exposure to professional concerns through similar access to conferences, meetings, newsletters, and journals).

STUDIES ON INNOVATION

The field of innovation is very broad and has been studied from many perspectives. Rogers' (1962) book, *The Diffusion of Innovations*, was perhaps one of the first attempts at a comprehensive review of innovation literature which employed an interdisciplinary approach. Miles' (1964) edited book on *Innovation in Education* is also a useful reference work because it deals specifically with theories and research on educational innovations. Other important early works in the field of innovation include collections of papers by Bennis, Benne, and Chin (1962) on *The Planning of Change* and by Goodwin Watson (1967a, 1967b) on *Concepts for Social Change* and *Change in School Systems*. In addition, an annotated bibliography about knowledge utilization has been produced by the Human Interaction Research Institute (Glaser 1976).

These works are all major contributions to the field of innovation, but they are not as specific to an organizational perspective as works by Havelock (1971) and Zaltman, Duncan, and Holbek (1973). These two major works along with several other recent studies pertain directly to innovation and organizations and offer both theoretical and practical ideas about the relationship of organizational characteristics to the adoption of innovation and will be considered in the subsections that follow.

Havelock

A major work in the area of innovation is Havelock's *Planning for Innovation Through Dissemination and Utilization of Knowledge* (1971). Done in collaboration with others at the center for Research on Utilization of Scientific Knowledge, this report provides a framework for understanding innovation. In discussing the factors which facilitate or inhibit the flow of information through organizations, Havelock utilizes three categories to describe organizational knowledge flow. These are entering (input), internal processing (throughput), and exiting (output).

In addition to these categories, Havelock made a distinction between maintenance information and new information. Most of the information people in organizations send and receive is not new information; it is maintenance information. The information is usually routine and often it is redundant. This kind of information is usually referred to as the communication pattern of the organization, but it is not necessarily true that what happens to maintenance information is the same for new information. New information is knowledge about new ideas and innovations; it is often research-based knowledge. Because the present study focuses on the utilization of a recommendation from research, the following discussion is limited to new information.

Havelock compares the organization to a giant egg encased in many shells, which are permeable under the right conditions. Each of the shells has the purpose of protecting the egg from the environment, particularly from hostile parts of the environment. Havelock identifies four specific shells that all organizations are likely to possess. These are the shells of survival, stability, purpose, and membership.

Survival is critical to all organizations. Some messages from the outside mean the end of an organization by exploitation, subversion, contamination, or takeover, and organizations maintain barriers to filter out these kinds of messages.

Stability is important to organizations in order for them to carry out their function in a predictable manner. In order to maintain their equilibrium, organizations must screen new information. Purpose is what binds an organization together, and organizations must erect barriers to keep out information that is irrelevant and might change their purpose. Membership also creates barriers to outside influences because all the attributes that unite members, such as common language, values, ideology, and roles, are the same attributes that set them apart from the rest of the world.

Using the recurring ideas of the four shells of survival, stability, purpose, and membership, Havelock reviews the previous literature on how knowledge flows into an organization and categorizes it into sets of factors that inhibit knowledge inflow and factors that facilitate it. The inhibitors are the need for stability, coding scheme barriers, social relationships, fear of malevolence of outsiders, personal threat, local pride, status difference among organizations, economic condition, training newcomers to accept the old ways, and size. The twelve facilitators are mechanisms that the organization uses to overcome barriers and inhibitors: reward value, change of leadership, perception of crises, examining other organizations, awareness, training, capacity, external agent, organizational invaders, importing human resources, knowledge-seeking subunits, and professionalism.

Output is very similar to input because it also concerns the shells of the organization. In order for knowledge to leave an organization, it must penetrate the shells of survival, stability, purpose, and membership. Although the processes involved in output are analogous to input processes, there are differences because output is crucial to an organization's existence. Organizational output is the means by which organizational effectiveness is measured. It seems contradictory that organizations possess characteristics which inhibit their mission of providing output, but the fact remains that there are organizational factors that inhibit output and factors that facilitate it.

The inhibitors of output are the need for stability, inertia, complacency or local pride, perceived vulnerability, goal definition, perceived client readiness, and professed danger to clients. The facilitators of output are competition, crises, affluence and capacity, internal openness, values supportive of quality output, specialized output roles, and subsystems.

Following a discussion of how new knowledge penetrates the shells of an organization through input and output, it is also important to look at how it moves through organizations. If the assumption is made that knowledge has entered an organization, one needs to examine the factors that influence whether it is utilized or not.

Internally every organization has other barriers or filters similar to the shells Havelock discussed earlier. Although there are also other organizational characteristics (innovation-suppressive reward patterns, type of training, physical separation, and traditional patterns of leadership) that inhibit how new knowledge flows through organizations, Havelock believes the chief factors in internal inhibitors are structural. These structural factors are the division of labor, the designation of specialized roles, and the ordering of roles in a structured hierarchy.

Division of labor or how each person or unit contributes to an organization can influence how messages flow in organizations. Division of labor creates separateness which can cause problems in three ways. It encourages the formation of unique vocabularies or coding schemes because of specialized concerns and interests. Jackson (1959) believes that division of labor occurs because of a natural desire to maintain the uniqueness and cohesiveness of the subgroup and points out that subunits almost become subcultures. Competition for resources is also evident in division of labor and can separate subunits both psychologically and sociologically. Beyond these differences in vocabulary and the effects in competition, separate subgroup norms and values also develop. Schein (1965) discusses the recurring problem with different subgroup norms when interdisciplinary committees are formed.

The designation of specialized roles is a necessary division of labor. Role expectations, however, which are designed to routinize behavior, usually encourage conformity and are so limited that there is little room for new ideas. Roles could also potentially facilitate knowledge transfer, particularly if knowledge transfer is the role expectation; unfortunately very few "knowledge-linking" roles exist within organizations.

The ordering of roles in a structural hierarchy is essential to any organization but this ordering can also inhibit new knowledge. Several authors such as Blau (1955), Griffiths (1964), and Burns and Stalker (1961) have discussed these impeding effects of hierarchical structure. Griffiths, who discusses organizational change in elementary schools, sums these ideas up by stating that the more hierarchical the structure of an organization is, the less likely change will occur. Hierarchical structures create barriers to knowledge flow through an organization.

Centralization, Havelock points out, is another aspect of structured hierarchy that can inhibit new ideas. Although it has been assumed that greater centralization will bring about more efficiency, this is not always the case. The inertia of large centralized school systems is a case in point. Centralization seems to improve downward communication, but the generation of new ideas and creativity are blocked in the most efficient systems.

Havelock also discusses twelve possible strategies for facilitating input: (1) developing a new style of leadership, which includes a mix of technical, organization, and human relations; (2) conducting organizational development training programs; (3) developing shared perceptions and superordinate goals with which all organizational subunits could identify; (4) increasing genuine participation and influence sharing up and down the hierarchy; (5) building overlapping subunits with multiple shared memberships; (6) providing for periodic job rotation; (7) creating specialists in the linking process; (8) restructuring itself; (9) decentralizing the organization; (10) changing the spatial arrangement of the organization; (11) changing the work flow patterns; and (12) rewarding desired behavior. Of these twelve facilitators, structural possibilities for change include adding specialists in the linking process in order to change the knowledge flow network and increasing the average span of control so that the number of relationships is increased within an organization.

Havelock (1971) argues for the inclusion of organizational factors in his framework for understanding innovation. His distinction between maintenance information and new information is very relevant to a study of research utilization, since it concerns new information from a research recommendation. In addition, the categories of input, output, and throughput are important to learning more about how a research recommendation enters and is utilized by an organization. Although Havelock does not confine his ideas to organizational structure factors, organizational structure is a key factor in his description of the flow of new knowledge in organizations. Havelock calls for more studies about organizational factors such as structure and their relationship to innovation.

Zaltman, Duncan, and Holbek

Another major review of innovation and organizations was done by Zaltman, Duncan, and Holbek (1973). The impetus for their book came from their frustration about a lack of information on the adoption of innovations in organizations. The chapter on organizational structure and innovation in which the authors describe the characteristics of complexity, formalization, and centralization, is particularly relevant to the current study.

Using the definition of complexity as the number of occupational specialties in the organization, Zaltman, Duncan, and Holbek (1973) discuss the positive and negative effects that the degree of complexity can have on the innovation process. A high number of specialties results in a great value being placed on specific knowledge and information, and the diversity of backgrounds increases the different types of information available to the organization. More innovations are conceived and proposed in complex organizations (Pelz and Andrews 1966); however it is also pointed out that there is likely to be more conflict in organizations that are highly complex. The authors cite Wilson's argument (1966), which points out the difficulties that any one group or individual has in trying to force consensus about adopting a proposal. It seems that at the initiation stage highly complex organizations are able to generate more knowledge and increase proposals for innovation, but at the implementation stage, high complexity makes it difficult for organizations to implement innovations.

Defining formalization as the emphasis placed on following specific rules and procedures in performing one's job, Zaltman, Duncan, and Holbek (1973) also see positive and negative effects of the degree of formalization on the innovation process. The assumption is usually made that emphasis on strict rules inhibits the innovation process, but it is again important to consider the stage of the process. Shepard (1967) has pointed out that low formalization may increase innovations during the initiation stage where the organization needs to be as flexible and open to new sources of information as possible; however, during the implementation stage, a singleness of purpose is needed and high formalization may increase the adoption of innovation.

Zaltman, Duncan, and Holbek (1973) define centralization as where the locus of authority is in the organization. The higher in the organization that decision making takes place, the greater the centralization and vice versa. A high degree of centralization usually means new information and channels of communication are restricted, and thus the innovation process is inhibited by high centralization. Again, however, the stage of the innovation process is important. In the initiation stage, it is important to have broad participation in order to get the most and best ideas. In the implementation stage, clear lines of authority are very important, and more innovations can be adopted when the organization is highly centralized. Lawrence and Lorsch's (1967) study is used as support for this argument because Lawrence and Lorsch found that in effective organizations, the fundamental research groups have the least structure and the production units are most structured.

Other Studies

Gross, Giacquinta, and Bernstein (1971) focus on the problems of implementing organizational innovations. They had serious reservations about the "overcoming initial resistance to change" explanation of the success or failure of an organization to implement change. Thus they examined an organization whose members were not initially resistant to change.

Gross, Giacquinta, and Bernstein (1971) argue for the inclusion of an organization variable in the theoretical formulations about the implementation of innovation. The innovation they studied was a change from the traditional role of elementary teacher as director of student learning, one who imparts a specific, predetermined standard set of curricula to students. The innovation called for the teacher to provide catalysts to learning, to guide students in problem solving, to be a role model, to be flexible, and to stress creativity. In their case study, they found that the organizational arrangements of the school that existed during the adoption of the innovation process were totally incompatible with the innovation. The examples of organizational barriers they used were rigid school schedules, which would not allow for the flexibility the innovation demanded, and the school's grading system, which required teachers to give letter grades at specific times. Both of these are examples of high formalization and are completely incompatible with the nature of the innovation. The authors call for more studies about the relationship of organizational factors to innovation adoption.

Baldridge (1975) reports on studies from the Stanford Center for Research and Development in Teaching. He argues that traditional research on innovation and organizational change have focused too narrowly on individual variables, small-scale innovations, and the early stages of innovation. He suggests that more attention needs to be paid to organizational and environmental features of the organization.

Baldridge (1975) provides evidence from two different Stanford studies that a size and complexity factor were positively related to innovation. He suggests that more role specialization, the creation of specialized positions, will facilitate innovation, and this, of course, is most often possible in large school districts. In addition, Baldridge points out that rapidly changing environments cause increased diversity and uncertainty and thus call for immediate action from an organization. This action is often in the form of an innovation.

Daft and Becker (1978) add another important idea about innovation in their longitudinal study of thirteen Illinois high school districts. Although they hypothesized the relationship of a variety of organizational variables to the adoption of innovations, strong relationships were not found. What Daft and Becker did find, however, was that there were different types of innovation and different innovation attributes.

Daft and Becker (1978) define type of innovation as members of a class and attribute as a characteristic of a member of a class. Their research differentiated between administrative and educational innovations. The importance of the group served was also an important distinction. Innovations can also differ on a variety of attributes such as cost, radicalness, compatibility, risk or profit potential. Daft and Becker (1978) suggest that researchers need to look at the specific attributes of individual innovations rather than aggregating all kinds of innovations into a single dependent variable.

CURRENT CONCERNS

In summary, the literature on research utilization and innovation leaves many unanswered questions, some of which this study attempts to address. In both the research utilization and innovation literature, it is apparent that more studies about the importance of organizational characteristics are needed.

The current concerns about utilization of a research recommendation are as follows:

1. Organizational theory has not been adequately considered in this particular area of innovation based on utilization of a research recommendation.
2. The definition of utilization needs to be broad and include both instrumental and conceptual utilization.
3. More studies using quantitative methodologies need to be done, particularly in one content area.
4. A present-time orientation needs to be considered rather than retrospective, hypothetical, or future orientations.
5. Organizational variables in the setting category need to be further delineated.

The current case study of Costin's recommendation (1969a) lessens some of the limitations of previous research by using organizational theory and including both instrumental and conceptual use in the definition of research utilization in the current study. In addition to using a quantitative methodology, the focus of the current study is on a present-time orientation, and the emphasis is on organizational structure variables in selected public school districts. Specifically, the present study tests the theory that there is a relationship between the organizational structure of public school districts and the utilization of a recommendation for change in social service delivery methods by Costin (1969a) in the area of school social work delivery.

The innovation literature calls for more studies about organizational factors and their relationship to new information. It calls for more studies about stages of the innovation process and characteristics of the innovation. Utilization of a research recommendation for a change in social service delivery methods is a particular kind of new information, an innovation based on research from outside the organization that calls for change within the organization. The current study considers these concerns.

The next chapter delineates the organizational perspective which the current study uses. It will provide general background on organizational theory as well as the specific theory on which this study is based.

3   Theoretical Context of the Study: Organizational Factors

The following overview of organizational theory is designed to present the theoretical perspective of the current study. In testing the theory that there is a relationship between organizational structure and the utilization of a research recommendation, I employ a sociological frame of reference where the organization is seen as a collective of roles rather than as an aggregate of individuals. Utilization of a research recommendation is examined in terms of general organizational utilization and not in terms of utilization by individuals.

Katz and Kahn (1966) provide a concise description of an organizational perspective. They state:

The major error in dealing with problems of organizational change, both at the practical and theoretical level, is to disregard the systemic properties of the organization and to confuse individual change with modifications in organizational variables. It is common practice to pull foremen or officials out of their organizational roles and give them training in human relations. Then they return to their customary positions with the same role expectations from their subordinates, the same pressures from their superiors, and the same functions to perform as before their special training. Even if the training program has begun to produce a different orientation toward other people on the part of the trainees, they are likely to find little opportunity to express their new orientation in the ongoing structured situation to which they return (p. 390).

The current study follows from the work of Hage and Aiken (1970), which stresses the importance of structural characteristics of formal organizations to the process of program change. The next subsections will briefly survey the general background work on the relationship of formal organizational structure characteristics to program change and show how the current study utilizes organizational theory as its conceptual framework.

BACKGROUND

Because we live in an "organizational society" (Etzioni 1964), much has been studied and written about organizations. There are a multiplicity of approaches from many disciplines which examine organizations. Gouldner (1959) developed a way of organizing these diverse approaches which was later extended by Thompson (1967). According to Gouldner and Thompson there are two major subsets of organizational theory: rational (closed) approaches and natural system (open) approaches. Although any classification of a particular theory is likely to receive support from some and disagreement from others, it is necessary to make some distinctions in order to understand the major trends in organizational theory.

In the rational approach, the organization is seen as an instrument that is rationally conceived and the organization is the means by which clearly announced group goals can be realized. Organizational structures are the tools by which organizations are administered, and changes in patterns of organizational structure are seen as planned devices. The focus is on rationality, deliberate actions, and formal patterns of operation, almost in a mechanical sense. Within the rational approach, there are classical and modern structural theories.

The classical or traditional structural theories in the rational model are represented by Frederick Taylor (1911) and others of the scientific management school. Economic efficiency was the ultimate goal, and it was sought by applying technical logic and setting standards for the organization. Luther Gulick and Lyndall Urwick (1937) are also part of the classical tradition from an administrative management perspective. Efficiency was again the ultimate goal, and it was maximized by departmentalization and task specialization. Probably the best known of the classical theorists is Max Weber and his theory of bureaucracy. Weber (1947) conceptualized bureaucracy as an ideal or "pure form" of organizational arrangement. Bureaucracy, according to Weber, was capable of attaining the maximum amount of efficiency. The essential elements of Weber's bureaucracy were division of labor, hierarchy of positions, technical qualifications, rule observation, and impersonality (cited in Wren 1972).

Modern structuralists such as Robert Merton suggest theories which look at the dysfunctions of bureaucracy. Merton (1960) posits that Weber did not recognize or deal with the limits which are related to the attainment of rationality and efficiency. For example, an overemphasis on discipline and rules can lead to replacement of goals with rigid rule observation; the means become the end, and there is goal displacement.

In the natural system approach, the organization is seen as a whole composed of interdependent parts. The organization is viewed as continually involved in processes related to survival, and people in roles are engaging in adaptive behavior in order to maintain their roles. Structures of organizations are seen as spontaneously maintained; changes are considered to be unplanned, adaptive responses. Human relations theories and contingency theories are two major divisions of the natural system (open) approach.

Human relations theories focus on individual differences, and their major emphasis is on the employee's motivation and satisfaction. They emerged largely as a reaction to the rational approach and the scientific management groups, which looked at men as machines. The work of Elton Mayo and his associates at the Western Electric Company in Chicago (the Hawthorne studies) showed the importance of the small group. Others in this tradition such as Argyris (1957), McGregor (1960), and Likert (1961) stressed the culture of the organization.

James Thompson (1967) is the best example of a contingency theorist. He proposed that the organization was always problem facing and problem solving. He saw organizations as attempting to be rational, but never being able to achieve this completely because of uncertainty. Other examples of contingency theories can be found in the work of Lawrence and Lorsch (1967) and Hall (1972).

HAGE AND AIKEN'S THEORY

Jerald Hage and Michael Aiken in their book *Social Change in Complex Organizations* (1970) present the theory that organizational characteristics are associated with program change. They base their theory on Hage's axiomatic theory (1965) and on their own research in sixteen welfare agencies (1967), which tested part of the axiomatic theory in relation to program change. The axiomatic theory has also been tested in the junior college milieu (Snead 1967) and in public school districts (Johnson 1978, Reeves 1978, and Thacker 1978).

Hage's axiomatic theory (1965) relates eight variables to each other in seven central propositions. Twenty-one corollaries can then be derived from these seven propositions. The eighth proposition is a limits theorem. It is a rational (closed) approach to organizations. The propositions and corollaries are listed in Table 3.1 and Table 3.2.

Hage and Aiken (1967) tested part of Hage's axiomatic theory, which related to adaptiveness or program change, in their study of sixteen social welfare agencies in the Midwest. It was hypothesized, based on the axiomatic theory, that the rate of program change was positively related to the degree of complexity and job satisfaction and negatively related to the degree of centralization and formalization. Interviews were conducted with the 314 staff members of the sixteen organizations, and it was found that complexity and job satisfaction were associated with high rates of program change and that centralization and for- malization were associated with low rates of program change. The analysis of data also showed that the number of occupational specialties was a better em- pirical indicator of program change than professional training or professional activities. Participation in decision making was also a better predictor of program change than degree of hierarchy of authority, and job codification was a better predictor of program change than rule observation.

Hage and Aiken's (1970) theory about the relationship of organizational char- acteristics to program change presents seven hypotheses that relate program

Table 3.1
Propositions of the Axiomatic Theory

Major Propositions

    I. The higher the centralization, the higher the production.

    II. The higher the formalization, the higher the efficiency.

    III. The higher the centralization, the higher the formalization.

    IV. The higher the stratification, the lower the job satisfaction.

    V. The higher the stratification, the higher the production.

    VI. The higher the stratification, the lower the adaptiveness.

    VII. The higher the complexity, the lower the centralization.

Limits Proposition

    VIII. Production imposes limits on complexity, centralization, formalization,

              stratification, adaptiveness, efficiency, and job satisfaction.

Source: Administrative Science Quarterly, 1965, *10*, 289–321.

change to one of the other seven organizational characteristics. These hypotheses are as follows:

1. The greater the complexity, the greater the rate of program change.
2. The higher the centralization, the lower the rate of program change.
3. The greater the formalization, the lower the rate of program change.
4. The greater the stratification, the lower the rate of program change.
5. The higher the volume of production, the lower the rate of program change.
6. The greater the emphasis on efficiency, the lower the rate of program change.
7. The higher the job satisfaction, the greater the rate of program change.

For each hypothesis they provide a rationale and examples from their earlier work or the work of others in closely related fields. Since the present study will consider only structural characteristics, the discussion will be limited to their

Table 3.2
Derived Corollaries of the Axiomatic Theory

1. The higher the formalization, the higher the production.

2. The higher the centralization, the higher the efficiency.

3. The lower the job satisfaction, the higher the production.

4. The lower the job satisfaction, the lower the adaptiveness.

5. The higher the production, the lower the adaptiveness.

6. The higher the complexity, the lower the production.

7. The higher the complexity, the lower the formalization.

8. The higher the production, the higher the efficiency.

9. The higher the stratification, the higher the formalization.

10. The higher the efficiency, the lower the complexity.

11. The higher the centralization, the lower the job satisfaction.

12. The higher the centralization, the lower the adaptiveness.

13. The higher the stratification, the lower the complexity.

14. The higher the complexity, the higher the job satisfaction.

15. The lower the complexity, the lower the adaptiveness.

16. The higher the stratification, the higher the efficiency.

17. The higher the efficiency, the lower the job satisfaction.

18. The higher the efficiency, the lower the adaptiveness.

19. The higher the centralization, the higher the stratification.

20. The higher the formalization, the lower the job satisfaction.

21. The higher the formalization, the lower the adaptiveness.

Source: Administrative Science Quarterly, 1965, *10*, 289–321.

ideas on complexity, centralization, formalization, and stratification (the first four hypotheses).

Complexity

Hage and Aiken (1970) define complexity as the level of knowledge and expertise in an organization. They look at both number of occupational specialties and the degree of professionalism in each as measures of complexity. They believe that the sheer number of occupations can lead to more change because there are more diverse perspectives and different values within the organization. As each occupation strives to achieve its fair amount of organizational power, more ways of improving performance and more new programs arise. The degree of professionalism is important because the more emphasis an organization places on knowledge, the more likely employees will keep abreast of new developments in the field and will want program changes.

Centralization

Centralization is defined by Hage and Aiken (1970) to be the way power is distributed in the organization. They believe that the more power is concentrated in the hands of a few people (high centralization), the more likely little change will take place, because of fear of changing the status quo. On the other hand, when an organization is less centralized and gives people from different occupations decision-making power, there is an interplay of new ideas which leads to program change.

Formalization

Hage and Aiken (1970) define formalization as the degree of job codification in an organization. The greater the number of rules usually means the greater formalization of the organization and the less likely program change will occur. They believe rules limit both what people do and what they think. High formalization does not encourage new progress.

Stratification

Stratification is defined by Hage and Aiken (1970) to be the differential distribution of rewards to jobs in an organization. These rewards are usually in the form of money or prestige. Hage and Aiken believe that those who have the most wealth and prestige are less likely to favor new programs if the changes might lessen their own status in any way. On the other hand, when there is very little difference in rewards, people tend to be more willing to communicate new ideas and new programs. There is more to be gained from program change when there is less stratification.

PRESENT INVESTIGATION

Hage and Aiken's work (1970) related program change to seven organizational characteristics. The present study hopes to extend Hage and Aiken's theory about the association between organizational characteristics and program change to include an association between organizational characteristics and the utilization of a research recommendation. Organizational characteristics are limited in the current study to include only the structural characteristics of complexity, centralization, formalization, and stratification.

The current investigation also uses a rational (closed) approach to organizations just as Hage did in the axiomatic theory of organizations. In accord with Gouldner (1959), I believe that it is crucial not to overlook the distinctive characteristics of modern organizations which make them rational bureaucracies. While acknowledging the contributions of the natural system approach, Gouldner stressed the importance of a systematic analysis of the parts of an organization in order to examine their functional autonomy.

Hage and Aiken also acknowledged the possible influences of environmental variables, but they did not think their influence would affect the direction of the hypothesized relationships. In a study of the axiomatic theory in public school districts (Johnson 1978, Reeves 1978, Thacker 1978) it was found that district size and wealth were significant environmental influences. Because of this possibility, several environmental factors will also be considered as control variables in the current study in order to identify possible confounding influences from the environment.

Chapter 2 reviewed the literature on research utilization and innovation and showed how a significant gap exists in the conceptualization of research utilization. This chapter has surveyed organizational theory and shown how the current study utilizes organizational theory as its conceptual framework.

1. The organization is seen as a collective of roles.

2. The organization is rationally conceived.

3. The organization is the means by which group goals can be realized.

4. Organizational structures are the tools by which organizations are administered.

5. Change is viewed as planned change.

The next chapters will describe the case study of school social work. Chapter 4 describes the historical background of the problem.

PART II

CASE EXAMPLE:
SCHOOL SOCIAL WORK

4 Historical Background of School Social Work

The issue of the most effective way to provide social services in the public schools has plagued school social workers since the turn of the century. This question remains inextricably related to the goal of school social work. In 1968 Prof. Lela Costin of the University of Illinois surveyed a national sample of school social workers about the content of their practice (their role) and the relative importance of the parts of their practice (their goal). The key recommendation which followed from her research was that the traditional casework emphasis in school social work practice was outmoded. A new approach—which looked at the whole school, at target groups of students, and at the relationships among home, school, and community—was needed.

Costin's recommendation was for a change in the social service delivery approach used by school social workers. The home, school, and community were all to be active participants in the educational process, and the school social worker was to play a redefined and more active role with administrators on policy issues (Costin 1969a). Costin advocated a changed goal for school social workers, which focused on the school as part of a larger social system and utilized the school social worker in a process of both system and institutional change.

In 1975, seven years after Costin's research, Meares (1977) replicated Costin's study using another national sample of school social workers and found that there had only been a modest change from the traditional form of school social work, casework to individual students, to Costin's recommended approach. Despite the fact that Costin believed casework was not meeting the needs of the public school, Meares did not find overwhelming acceptance of Costin's new approach. What Meares did find was a range of responses. Some school social workers reported primarily a casework approach while others reported the adoption of Costin's recommendation. Many school social workers, however, reported a transitional role between the polar extremes of a casework approach and Costin's approach. More recently, adaptations and partial uses of Costin's approach are evident in the reports of an increase in multidisciplinary team and teacher consultation activities (Parr & Alstein 1979, Timberlake, Sabatino, & Hooper 1982). The utilization of Costin's recommendation can at best be described as uneven.

In order to understand the evolution of the issues involved in the utilization of Costin's recommendation, it is important to look at the historical background of the goal of school social work. I examine three major time periods: 1890–1930, the beginnings of school social work; 1930–1960, casework emphasis; and 1960–1980, era of change.

1890–1930: THE BEGINNINGS OF SCHOOL SOCIAL WORK

School social work originated outside the school system with close ties to the settlement house movement, civic associations, and private philanthropy. In 1906 in New York City, four settlement houses joined together to sponsor two home visitors for three school districts. Visiting teachers did not like the status of informal affiliation with schools; they desired full and official status. By 1913 this status was conferred in both New York City and Rochester, New York, schools. From its meager beginnings in three school districts in New York City, by the 1920s school social workers had expanded all over the East and Midwest, with the assistance of private organizations such as the Boston Home and School Association, the West End Neighborhood Association (Boston), the Hartford Psychological Clinic, the Child Welfare Committee of the friends Quarterly Meeting (Philadelphia), and the Chicago Women's Club (Oppenheimer 1924, Lubove 1973).

The first national conference of school social work was held in conjunction with the National Education Association in 1916 and the second in conjunction with the National Conference of Social Work in 1919 (Lide 1953). In 1921 the National Association of Visiting Teachers held its own conference. At about the same time the Commonwealth Fund in its program for prevention of delinquency was supporting visiting teachers in thirty communities. From 1921–24, the Commonwealth Fund subsidized visiting teachers, developed courses of training for visiting teachers, and disseminated the benefits of visiting teachers to educators and communities (Oppenheimer 1924).

Education in this period was highly influenced by the ideas of John Dewey (1902). In larger cities there were also close ties to the settlement house movement as is evidenced by the establishment of the first settlement house kindergarten as early as 1887. Many of the early settlement house residents were educators both by instinct and by training (Woods & Kennedy 1922). The Speyer School Settlement and School Social Center in New York City in 1902 was an example of teachers and social workers living and learning practical education. The schools were often used as general community centers for all ages, an approach strongly supported by Mary Follett (1924).

An important educational development during this period was compulsory attendance. Although by no means uniform across the states, compulsory attendance laws began to appear on the books. However, as Edith Abbott and Sophonisba P. Breckinridge suggested in their study of nonattendance in the Chicago schools in 1917, legislation was not enough to meet the social needs of children. Truant officers could only return children to school; they could do nothing about the causes of nonattendance (Abbott & Breckinridge, 1917).

Along with compulsory attendance came the problem of how to deal with the many different kinds of children who were now required to attend school. The schools, in a search to find ways to deal with the mentally handicapped, the delinquent, and the culturally different child, developed an interest in scientific measures of education. The "orgy" of tabulation began, and a new emphasis was placed on efficiency in school administration and standardized training and certification (Cremin 1961, Bremner 1971, Vol. 2).

The period of 1890–1930 was a period of rapid growth for both education and social work. Both were influenced by the progressive and social reform views that human suffering was neither the fault nor the destiny of the individual and that much of the suffering could be prevented through education. Progressive education began as an effort to improve the lives of individuals; children, in particular, were seen as the key for the solution of the problems of urban life. Societal needs were apparent, and school social work emerged as part of this new perspective on poverty and child development. The school was a tool for acculturation, because it reached the majority of children and might ensure the nurturing of a respectable future generation. The school aided immigration by providing services and preparing children for Americanization by exposing them to a common education (Lubove 1973).

Social work was very much a part of the new social conscience, this new view on poverty and child development. The old friendly visitor idea of the charity organization societies was incompatible with a new focus on environmental causation. Poverty was widespread and was working-class poverty as opposed to dependent poverty. Moral superiority had no place in the new world of scientific philanthropy. The answer for social work was in a professional relationship with clients where the emphasis was on superior skills and expertise, not superior class (Richmond 1917, Lubove 1973).

During this period the goal of school social work focused on bringing the home and school closer together. The principal methods of social service delivery were teachers' conferences and home visits, and the focus was on improving attendance, scholarship, and home conditions.

1930–1960: CASEWORK EMPHASIS

The depression affected school social work tremendously. During the decade of the thirties, a time that should have been a continuation of the expansion of school social work, there was a general cutback of services. School social work was seen as a luxury service (Areson 1933). When the depression eased and the schools resumed hiring social workers, priorities shifted from serving poor, delinquent, and truant children to serving middle-class children with emotional or learning problems. Edith Everett (1938) stated that school social work must limit its professional responsibility to casework and forget about the broader community. The casework emphasis is evident in 1956 in the guide to curriculum content in school social work, which was published by the National Association of Social Workers, and in articles on the implications of psychiatry for school social work practice (Coleman 1951, Altmeyer 1956, Mitchell 1957, Beck 1958, Schour 1958, Walker 1958).

Education from 1930–1960 also underwent changes from the depression. The schools, the teachers, and the students were all victims of the depression, but there were counterforces that affected it simultaneously and helped education remain strong. The crisis in employment made it desirable to remain in school; the Roosevelt administration provided loans to pay teachers' salaries; the Public Works Administration and the Works Progress Administration provided new school construction (Bremner 1971, Vol. 3).

Educational philosophy and treatment of minority groups also were re-examined during this period. The migration of African-Americans from the South during the 1940s and 1950s brought racism out into the open. Since 1896 the Plessy v. Ferguson decision had protected legal segregation. Very little attention was paid to discrimination until Brown v. the Board of Education of Topeka in 1954. Another revision of educational philosophy came with the launching of the Sputnik satellite in 1957 by the Soviet Union. A high premium was placed on science, mathematics, and foreign language education, and in 1958 the National Defense Education Act was passed, which authorized large amounts of funds for those subject areas (Bremner 1971, Vol. 3).

The general profession of social work followed in being affected by the depression. Attitudes toward relief shifted to express a concern that aid should be public rather than private and that the federal government should go beyond merely advising the states. The 1935 Social Security Act created huge new bureaucracies in the areas of federal social insurance, unemployment insurance, and public welfare, but social workers were not the rank and file workers in these agencies. When social workers were present, they were supervisors and administrators (Leiby 1978). The mainstream of social work, however, remained in the voluntary, nongovernmental sector with an emphasis on personal counseling or casework.

The historical developments in school social work and education had a strong relationship to the issue of the goal of the school social worker. It was at this time that a major split became obvious and resulted in the dominance of casework over the community-oriented approach. School social work focused more on the middle class during the period from 1930–60 and tried to help the individual become better adjusted and effective (Guzzetta 1972). When school social work did work with truancy and delinquency, the emphasis was on the child's emotional development.

Edith Everett's 1938 assertion that school social work should accept existing school attendance laws and established scholastic standards portrayed the prevailing attitude about what the goal of school social work should be. It should not be based on social or institutional change, but rather on helping children to accept and achieve the standards and laws of schools and other institutions.

In accord with this changed goal, the tasks of school social workers were also different from those in the earlier period. Mildred Sikkema's 1953 *Report of a Study of School Social Work Practice in Twelve Communities* showed that a large proportion of referrals came from personality or behavior problems, and casework was the primary social service delivery method. This is very different from Oppenheimer's 1924 study of 1,300 records, where the most common referral was poor scholarship, and Culbert's 1929 report of 8,500 cases where over half of the referrals were for poor scholarship. It was also in direct contrast to Ellis's 1925 investigation of the visiting teacher in Rochester, where work upon home conditions far outnumbered any other type of social service delivery method.

The changed goal of school social work was also evident in the split relationship between the fields of education and social work in the period 1930–1960. The original home visitors were often former educators (with no special training or skills in social welfare) who saw their goal as community oriented. However, the desire to professionalize the school social worker resulted in social workers adopting a more scientific approach to social problems by the study of individual human behavior. The emphasis was on skilled casework, and this meant specialized training other than education training. It was during this period that accreditation of graduate schools of social work was established, with most students entering these programs directly from college (Lubove 1973).

The literature of the two periods reflects this split between a very congruent education and social work goal and more specialized, separate goals for social work and education. In 1914 at the National Education Association, Sophonisba Breckinridge spoke of the need for the visiting teacher to interpret the home to the school and the school to the home (Breckinridge 1914). In 1927, however, Howard Nudd, director of the Public Education Association of New York and chairman of the National Committee on Visiting Teachers, said that a visiting teacher's training had to include psychiatric and psychological principles, so that she would be able to understand the child's attitudes and characteristics (Nudd 1927).

Nudd's statement is representative of the divergence in social work and education goals that occurred during the period 1930–1960. Social work goals were directed toward a child's mental health; education goals were directed toward a child's mental abilities. Social workers were specially trained in mental health and teachers were specially trained in education. Social work believed it was on the path to professionalization by directing its attention to the psychiatric foundations of casework and dissociating itself from teaching. This change in the social work goal created "turf" issues, which resulted in education and social work becoming competing professionals in the thirties. The attitudes of the two groups focused on their separate identities and different roles within the school (Lubove 1973).

1960–1980: ERA OF CHANGE

The sixties were the beginnings of a new awareness for school social work. The literature reflects a questioning of the narrow treatment activities and goals of school social work. Proposals for new methods of practice were introduced. Arlien Johnson's 1962 book *School Social Work: Its Contribution to Professional Education* looks at the school as a social system, and collaboration between the profession of education and social work is emphasized (Johnson 1962). NASW established a committee on groupwork in the schools (Costin 1969b), and Vinter and Sarri (1965) presented a report of research that demonstrated the effectiveness of working with groups of students. The National Association of Social Workers (NASW) and the National Institute of Mental Health (NIMH) jointly sponsored a national workshop in 1969, "Social Change and School Social Work in the 1970's" where the major issues in education and their implications for school social work were discussed (Kahn 1972, Sarri 1972).

School social work was growing rapidly during this era of change. Hawkins (1979) reports that all fifty-one states (including the District of Columbia) employed school social workers and forty- two states (82.4%) certified school social work personnel. Graduate Schools of Social Work and Education were expanding to provide better training programs for social workers who worked in the schools, and states like Georgia and Pennsylvania developed interdisciplinary training programs to reflect the overlapping roles of pupil personnel workers.

Manpower issues were discussed at a workshop in Florida in 1971, where it was pointed out that there was no coherent pattern of service for employing school social workers (Guzzetta 1972). Four different models of school social work were identified and discussed by Alderson in 1972. Accountability to clients, employers, and professional associates is also discussed for the first time during this period (Anderson 1975). In 1978 the first NASW national school social work conference was held in Denver, Colorado, and in 1979 two new national journals on school social work were begun. NASW established a Special Committee on School Social Work in 1973, and by 1983 the NASW Board established school social work as a separate membership division.

Education also was in a period of transition and change from 1960–1980. Explosive growth was the most obvious development. In 1970, 75% of the young adults had at least a high school diploma; this was double the percentage in 1940. In addition, in 1970 nearly three times the number in 1940 had college degrees. The fathers of nearly two thirds of the 1970 college graduates had not gone beyond high school. The familiar generation gap might really have been an education gap (Bremner 1971, Vol. 3).

American education began to be compared with the educational accomplishments of other nations. Traditional separateness between nations was destroyed by depression, war, threat of nuclear annihilation, cold war, and Vietnam. The Soviet Sputnik had done much to foster new interest in what was happening in education. Increased funding came through the Elementary and Secondary Education Act in 1965 and in 1968. The Education for Handicapped Act of 1970 and the Education for All Handicapped Children Act of 1975 (P.L. 94-142) both had significant impacts on the direction of education. The Civil Rights Movement, the Coleman Report on the lack of equal educational opportunity, and a series of books by authors like Silberman (1970), Holt (1964, 1967), Kohl (1970), and Kozol (1967) all pointed to a need for reform. The youth of the nation were demanding change in education, and the school became the place to experiment with social change. As the school became the agent for reform, its very basis was reevaluated and its effectiveness was questioned.

The sixties were a time of change, social action, and human rights. Community organization advanced in this era; there was an anti-intellectualism trend, a push for relevancy, and a skepticism toward academia. During this period school social work was also changing its goals. The literature reflects a continual debate between the casework approach and other more change-oriented approaches which saw the school as part of a social system. The goal of serving individual students and meeting their emotional needs through intensive casework service was being challenged.

THE COSTIN STUDY

Costin's research (1969a) was conducted in the middle of the era of change. Her study sought to find out how school social workers defined their role and their goal. The research was conducted in 1968 and reported in 1969 in the *Social Service Review* ("An Analysis of the Tasks in School Social Work"). The research was financed in part by a grant from the United States Department of Health, Education, and Welfare, Office of Education. It is assumed to be methodologically sound research and is significant, because it was a pioneering national study of school social work. Professor Costin's research prompted many other studies of school social work and established her as a national leader in the field.

Costin began the study by assembling a list of tasks known to be contained in the professional activities of the school social worker and writing these in behavioral terms. The tasks were then translated into 107 items, and respondents were asked "How important do you consider the task for the attainment of social work goals within a school system?" A four-point rating scale from 0 (not important) to 3 (very important) was utilized. A list of school social workers was obtained from state departments of education, faculty members of graduate schools of social work, and known school social workers in supervisory positions. From a list of 1,456 school social workers in forty states and the District of

Columbia, a sample of 368 names was randomly selected. A total of 238 returned questionnaires were used in her analysis.

A factor analysis was used on the responses to the 107 items, and nine factors emerged: casework service to the child and his parents; caseload management; interpreting school social work service; clinical treatment of children with emotional problems; liaison between the family and community agencies; interpreting the child to the teacher; educational counseling with the child and his parents; leadership and policy-making; and personal service to the teacher.

To get a clearer perspective of what Costin found, the table which appeared in the *Social Service Review* article is provided. Table 4.1 presents the rank order of factor means for Costin's study.

On the basis of the responses to the question on the importance of the task to the attainment of social work goals within a school system, it was determined that school social workers in Costin's study assigned the most importance to the factor of casework service to the child and his parents. The factor of leadership and policy-making was assigned the least importance. Costin concluded that the definition of school social work's goal reflected the literature of the 1940s and 1950s. She felt it was not responding to the concerns of the 1960s or the underlying conditions in the school, neighborhood, and community. Costin believed that the definition of the goal of school social work was a static one and ignored the pressing problems of the school population, the social conditions underlying the problems, and the relationship of the school to the other social institutions in the community.

Costin made her recommendation for a new approach in social service delivery based on a combination of her research and her personal experience and beliefs. Her recommendation for change in service delivery included consultation with school administrators in formulation of administrative policy, consultation with teachers on general classroom issues, group work with students, work with parents on students' rights issues, and assistance in resource development and planned change in the community. These were her suggestions for bringing about change in the system of school-community-pupil relations. The goal of the new approach was to alleviate stress upon target groups of students and to facilitate the effective use of learning opportunities by all students.

Several related events provided the impetus for Costin's study and supported her recommendation for a change in social service delivery methods. The Kerner Commission placed some of the responsibility for violent conflicts between blacks and whites on the schools by suggesting that the schools had failed to provide appropriate education for all children (Report of the National Advisory Committee on Civil Disorder 1968). School conditions in the late sixties were unsettled and were characterized by racial and economic segregation of pupils, stereotyped views of the potential of disadvantaged students, the use of corporal punishment to control student behavior, and inadequate communication between the school and the community (Silberman 1970, Sarri 1972). Another related concern of the sixties was a shortage of social work manpower; there was an insufficient

Table 4.1
Rank Order of Factor Means

FACTOR	NUMBER OF TASKS	FACTOR MEAN*	STANDARD DEVIATION
2. Casework service to the child and his parents	13	2.90	.356
5. Caseload management	7	2.73	.549
6. Interpreting school social work service	8	2.72	.549
9. Clinical treatment of children with emotional problems	6	2.71	.537
7. Liaison between the family and community agencies	7	2.68	.541
8. Interpreting the child to the teacher	5	2.63	.591
3. Educational counseling with the child and his parents	12	2.31	.831
1. Leadership and policy-making	18	2.20	.846

*The means of factors differed significantly (that is, at the 5 percent level) with these exceptions: factors 5, 6, and 9; and factors 7 and 8 do not differ significantly.

Source: Social Service Review, 1960, 43, 277.

number of trained social workers in all areas of social welfare, including the school. Costin's recommendation was thus in accord with the times. Her approach focused on the whole school and attempted to change the pupil's environment, which is exactly what the Kerner Commission called for. Her approach also required less manpower, because it dealt with target groups of students and not individuals (Costin 1978). The civil rights legislation, the Office of Economic Opportunity (OEO) programs, the firm commitment to social responsibility through VISTA and the Peace Corps, and a growing volunteer segment of society all influenced and were in accord with Costin's recommendation (Pins 1966).

Costin's recommendation for a change in the goal and activities of school social work stimulated several other studies, which analyzed the tasks of school social workers and the importance of these tasks to the goal of school social workers. Alderson and Krisef (1973) found the opposite of Costin's results and reported that in their more limited sample; leadership and policy-making were rated high in the importance of tasks. Meares (1977) replicated Costin's study and found that school social work was slowly moving away from a casework approach to a transitional approach of home-school-community liaison and educational counseling. Meares's work is supported by Parr and Alstein's study (1979) of a parochial school setting, where there was a gradual shift away from casework to teacher consultation. Carr (1976), however, reported that 67% of the school social worker's time was still being utilized for direct services to individual pupils or their parents, and Flynn (1976) reported that casework services to children was given a high ranking in importance. Lambert and Mullaly (1982) found that school social workers recognized the importance of both individual casework and systems change. Timberlake, Sabatino, and Hooper (1982) found an increase in the practice dimensions of the multidisciplinary team, direct services, and data collection/information sharing since P.L. 94-142, the Education for All Handicapped Children Act of 1975.

It is clear that there has been an inconsistent pattern of utilization of Costin's recommendation; the goal of school social work varies from one district to another. Some districts have adopted the Costin recommendation, others have modified it, and still others have completely rejected it or may not even have considered it.

The next chapter will describe the procedures used in the current investigation, which tests the theory that there is a relationship between organizational structure and the utilization of a research recommendation.

5 *School Social Work Study*

A quantitative study that employs mailed questionnaires is used to examine the theory that there is a relationship between organizational structure and the utilization of a research recommendation. The study specifically examines the utilization of Costin's recommendation (1969a) in the field of school social work which suggested a changed goal for school social work and a change in the method of social service delivery. From the central problem of the study (why Costin's research recommendation was utilized in some school districts, adapted in some, and rejected or not considered in others), the following major question and five subquestions are addressed:

Major Question:

Is there a relationship between the organizational structure of public school districts and utilization of Costin's recommendation?

Subquestions:

1. Is there a relationship between the degree of complexity and utilization of Costin's recommendation?
2. Is there a relationship between the degree of centralization and utilization of Costin's recommendation?
3. Is there a relationship between the degree of formalization and utilization of Costin's recommendation?
4. Is there a relationship between the degree of stratification and utilization of Costin's recommendation?
5. Are the relationships between organizational structure variables and utilization of Costin's recommendation affected when district size, district resources, and district expenditures are controlled?

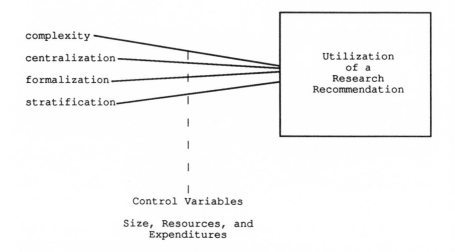

Figure 5.1 Summary of Variables

The research is schematically represented in Figure 5.1. The following sub-sections will describe the methodology of the study in more detail: the theoretical assumptions guiding the study, the working hypotheses, the variables and their measurement; the population and sample, the instruments, procedures for data collection, and procedures for data coding and analysis.

THEORETICAL ASSUMPTIONS

The study uses organizational theory, particularly the work of Hage and Aiken (1970), as its conceptual basis. It assumes that the organization is a collective of roles, is rationally conceived, and is the means by which group goals can be realized. Organizational structures are seen as tools by which organizations are administered, and change in the organization is viewed as planned change.

A sociological frame of reference is employed; the organization is the unit of analysis. The organization is viewed as an aggregate of roles rather than as a group of individuals. Utilization of the research recommendation will be examined in terms of general organizational utilization and not in terms of utilization by individuals.

THE WORKING HYPOTHESES

The predicted relationships between organizational structure variables and the utilization of Costin's research recommendation were logically derived from previous theory and empirical evidence. They parallel Hage and Aiken's predictions (1970) concerning structural variables and organizational adaptiveness discussed in Chapter 3.

Complexity

Complexity (the number of occupational specialties) is predicted to be positively related to utilization (both instrumental and conceptual) of a research recommendation. It is theorized that people with more specialized training take pride in their positions and their specialized tasks, and thus a positive climate for new ideas is created. Mort's work (cited in Ross 1958) found that the level of specialty training of teachers was highly correlated with the adoption of new teacher techniques. Similarly, a study by Hage and Aiken (1967) found that the number of occupational specialties in sixteen welfare agencies was positively related to the number of new programs added.

Hage and Aiken (1970) believed that the sheer number of occupations can lead to change because there are more diverse perspectives within the organization. They saw each occupation as striving to achieve and maintain its share of power by keeping abreast of new developments and trying new ways of doing things. In other words, Hage and Aiken (1970) believe that complexity promotes healthy competition.

Zaltman, Duncan, and Holbek's (1973) caution about the stage of the innovation process is also important. The utilization of a research recommendation from outside the organization must go through an initiation stage. The diversity in a large number of occupations facilitates awareness of research recommendations and increased awareness facilitates the opportunities for utilization. Complexity allows input into the organization (Havelock 1971).

In addition, Costin's recommendation is what Daft and Becker (1978) call an educational innovation that works best in organic structures, those that possess a bottom-up innovation process. A large number of professionals communicating and discussing their ideas increases the opportunity for utilization of the research recommendation.

Centralization

Centralization (the degree of influence in decision making that the superintendent—that is, the highest organizational position—has) is predicted to be inversely related to both instrumental and conceptual utilization of a research recommendation. The concentration of decision-making influence in a few top positions usually leads to preservation of the status quo. Change or new ideas are usually vetoed by the status quo because they might upset their present power system. V. Thompson (1965) suggests that centralization creates a psychological climate with an environment hostile to new ideas, and this view is supported by

Cillie's earlier work (1940), which showed that centralization was negatively related to experimentation in a study of New York City schools.

Hage and Aiken (1970) also believed that the more power is concentrated in the hands of a few people, the less likely change will take place. Conversely, when many people share in the decision-making process, there is likely to be a large pool of ideas and propensity to try new ideas. A high degree of authority by a few people frequently restricts communication among members and lessens the amount of information available to the organization, particularly what Havelock (1971) termed new information. Hage and Aiken strongly favored decentralized administrations.

The importance of time is again relevant in centralization (Zaltman, Duncan, & Holbeck 1973). When a school district is first considering the utilization of research recommendations, it is critical that the organization be decentralized, so that as many new insights and ideas as possible can be considered. Participation in the decision-making process can also increase organizational members' commitment to working through implementation difficulties. In accord with Daft and Becker (1978), utilization of Costin's recommendation is characterized by member involvement and relative freedom at lower organizational levels. Utilization of Costin's recommendation (1969a) demands a bottom-up innovation process, a district with low centralization.

Formalization

Formalization (the degree to which rules govern daily work) is predicted to be negatively related to both instrumental and conceptual research utilization. Rules are not conducive to the utilization of new ideas. According to Merton (1960) extreme formalization can result in ritualism or compulsive rule observation. Hage and Aiken's study (1967) also found that the number of regulations was negatively related with new programs. Hage and Aiken suggest that rules limit the amount and content of what people do and think. Rules do not encourage creativity or new ideas, which are necessary for innovation and utilization or research recommendations.

Strict emphasis on rules prohibits decision makers from seeking new information. There just is no time or opportunity to identify organizational problems and seek new solutions when there must be strict adherence to rules and procedures. Particularly in what Zaltman, Duncan, and Holbek (1973) call the initiation stage in the utilization of a research recommendation, it is important that there be flexibility and openness to new ideas. In addition, Costin's recommendation fits Daft and Becker's classification (1978) of an educational type of innovation that is adopted best in organizations that function from the bottom up, with a minimum of rules and much communication. Low formalization is necessary for utilization of Costin's recommendation.

Stratification

Stratification (difference in salaries between highest and lowest paid professional positions) is predicted to be inversely related to both instrumental and conceptual research utilization. Barnard (1946) states that high stratification is likely to be associated with little change because the people with the highest salaries are the ones potentially most affected by any organizational changes that might redistribute salary monies and thus are the most resistant. Barnard also argues that suggestions for change are both an implicit and explicit criticism of those who are currently on the top of the stratification hierarchy, because the present arrangements were most likely instituted by the people with the highest salaries; therefore a highly stratified system discourages change. Ben-David's historical analysis (1962) of medical research supports this idea; it shows that little change in medical developments occurred in countries where medical research was highly stratified.

Hage and Aiken (1970) also believe that those who have the most wealth and prestige are most likely to resist new programs because these changes might affect the current distribution of rewards from which they benefit. Those with high salaries and positions have the most to lose in organizational change. Conversely, when there is little difference in salaries or rewards, people tend to be creative more frequently and openly. Increased communication facilitates new ideas and the utilization of research.

Control Variables

Although they are not the major focus of the study, several control variables reflecting school district characteristics are included. These are district size, district resources, and district expenditures. It is predicted that these variables will affect the relationships between the organizational structure variables and utilization of a research recommendation (both instrumental and conceptual).

Size was found to be an important environmental factor in the relationship between organizational structure and district adaptability in the work of Johnson (1978), Reeves (1978), and Thacker (1978). Other studies by Mort (cited in Ross 1958) and Corwin (1972) have reported a relationship between size and organizational characteristics.

Johnson (1978), Reeves (1978), and Thacker (1978) also found district wealth to be an important factor in the relationship between organizational structure and district adaptability. Similarly, the work of Daft and Becker (1978) found slack resources to be an enabler variable that increased the probability of decisions in favor of the adoption of an innovation. Slack was defined as the disparity between the resources available to the school district and the payments required to maintain it. In the current study, district wealth is defined in two ways: district resources and district expenditures. This was done to see if there were any differences between districts that had wealth and spent it on their students and districts that had wealth and did not spend it on their students.

Because of this previous research, it is hypothesized that the control variables of district size, district resources, and district expenditures do affect the relationships between the organizational structure variables and utilization of Costin's research recommendation. No hypothesis about the strength or direction of these effects is offered at this time since the control variables are not a major focus of the study and previous studies are limited.

Summary

It should be noted that no attempt is made to establish cause and effect in this study; the nature of the methodology rules out making causal inferences. Rather, the present investigation tests the theory that there is a relationship between selected organizational structure variables (complexity, centralization, formalization, and stratification) and utilization of a research recommendation.

In summary, the hypothesized relationships between the organizational structure variables and the utilization of a research recommendation are in accord with Hage and Aiken's predictions (1970). The five hypotheses are these:

1. Complexity is positively related to the utilization of a research recommendation. The more occupational specialties, the more utilization of a research recommendation will occur. The fewer the occupational specialties, the less utilization of a research recommendation will occur.

2. Centralization is negatively related to utilization of a research recommendation. The larger the degree of influence that the highest level position has, the less utilization of a research recommendation will occur. The smaller the degree of influence that the highest level position has, the more utilization of a research recommendation will occur.

3. Formalization is negatively related to utilization of a research recommendation. The more that rules govern daily work, the less utilization of a research recommendation will occur. The less that rules govern daily work, the more utilization of a research recommendation will occur.

4. Stratification is negatively related to research utilization. The larger the difference in salaries, the less utilization of a research recommendation will occur. The smaller the difference in salaries, the more utilization of a research recommendation will occur.

5. The control variables of district size, district resources, and district expenditures will affect the relationships between the organizational structure variables and utilization of a research recommendation.

These hypotheses are the same for both instrumental and conceptual utilization of a research recommendation.

VARIABLES AND THEIR MEASUREMENT

The definition of organizational structure, the independent variable, is the same as Hage and Aiken's definition (1970) and includes four variables: complexity, centralization, formalization, and stratification. *Complexity* is the diversity of knowledge and expertise in an organization and is measured by the number of occupational specialties. *Centralization* is concerned with the way in which power is distributed and is measured by the degree of influence in decision making that the highest organizational position has. *Formalization* is the extent of job codification and is measured by the degree to which rules govern daily work and the job descriptions. *Stratification* refers to the differential distribution of rewards in an organization and is operationalized by the difference in salaries between the highest and lowest paid professional positions.

Utilization of a research recommendation, the dependent variable, means the extent to which the recommendation from the research is used. It is defined in two parts. *Instrumental utilization* means documented use; *conceptual utilization* means the research recommendation influenced thinking. The definition of *research recommendation* is further delimited by the fact that the recommendation comes from external research, research conducted by an outside agency or person, and by the fact that the recommendation is a change recommendation, a recommendation that might change the organization itself.

Three control variables are included: district size, district resources, and district expenditures. *District size* refers to student enrollment. *District resources* means the amount of money available to the district per pupil. *District expenditures* means the amount of money spent by the district per pupil.

Each of these variables and its specific operationalization for the current study is further described in the individual subsections that follow and in Figure 5.2. In addition, it is important to define several terms that will be used in conjunction with the measurement of the variables.

School district is the organizational division of public schools within a specified geographical region as determined by the state office of education. Superintendent is the chief administrator of the school district as defined by the state office of education. Supervisors are defined as state-certified professionals with B.A./B.S. or higher degrees, who are responsible for directing and evaluating one or more social workers in the district. School social workers are defined as state-certified professionals with B.A./B.S./B.S.W. or higher degrees, who are employed by public school districts to provide social services.

Complexity

Complexity, in accord with Hage and Aiken (1970), refers to the diversity of knowledge and expertise in the organization and is determined by the number of occupational specialties. In this study, a ratio of specialized personnel to other professional school personnel will be used as the indicator of complexity. Spe-

VARIABLE	TYPE	OPERATIONAL DEFINITION	HOW MEASURED	INFORMANT	CRITERIA
Complexity	Independent	Number of occupational specialities	Instrument #1 & #2	Superintendent & Supervisor	Ratio of non-classroom teacher professionals to all professionals in district
Centralization a) program policy b) work	Independent	Degree of superintendent's influence in decision-making about job description (program policy) and about daily social service delivery (work).	Instrument #1 & #2	Superintendent & Supervisor	Centralization scale about: a) program policy b) work
Formalization	Independent	Degree to which rules govern daily work	Instrument #1 & #2	Superintendent & Supervisor	Job Codification Scale
Stratification	Independent	Difference in salaries between highest and lowest paid position	Instrument #1 & #2	Superintendent & Supervisor	Difference in salaries between superintendent and entry-level, B.A. teachers

Utilization of a Research Recommendation: a) instrumental b) conceptual	Dependent	Degree to which research recommendation is used in activities performed (instrumental) and is specifically identified in the operational description of school social work (conceptual)	Instrument #3	Social Worker	Utilization score for eleven activities a) instrumental b) conceptual
District Size	Control	Student enrollment as of September 1982	Instrument #1 & #2	Superintendent & Supervisor	Factual response to question about student enrollment
District Resources	Control	Amount of money available to the district per pupil	1980 Annual Report form each state	State Office of Education	Rating of money available to the district per pupil (within each state)
District Expenditures	Control	Amount of money spent by the district per pupil	1980 Annual Report form each state	State Office of Education	Rating of money spent by district per pupil (within each state)

Figure 5.2 Measurement of Variables

cialized personnel will be defined as certified professionals (employees with B.A. or higher) who have a title other than classroom teacher. The higher the ratio is, the more complexity; the lower the ratio is, the less complexity. A ratio is used in order to account for differences in school district size since the number of specialized personnel is meaningless unless the total professional population is considered.

The ratio will be determined from two questions to the superintendent on mailed Instrument no. 1 (see Appendix A):

1. What is the total number of certified professionals (employees with a B.A. or more) currently employed by your district?

2. How many of the above certified professionals have job titles other than classroom teacher?

Centralization

Centralization is concerned with the way power is distributed and is defined in this study as the degree of influence that the highest organizational position has in decision making. The highest organizational position in the present inquiry is the superintendent, and thus a large degree of superintendent's influence in decision making means high centralization, and a small degree of superintendent's influence in decision making means low centralization. This definition follows Hage's work (1965), which defined centralization as the concentration of authority to make decisions in the hands of a few individuals. Perrow (1967), however, noted that because there were at least two kinds of decisions (about policy and about work), centralization should be measured in at least two ways. This study will employ a two-part definition where centralization related to program policy decisions means the degree of superintendent's influence in decision-making about program policy (job description) and where centralization related to work decisions means the degree of superintendent's influence in decision-making about work (social service delivery methods).

Perceived centralization about policy and about work will be measured by questions from Instrument no. 1 and Instrument no. 2 (see Appendix).

The question about program policy will be: How much influence or say does each of the following (superintendent, central office administrative staff, social work supervisor or immediate supervisor, and social worker) have on a decision about the content of the job description of the school social worker in your district?

The question about work will be: How much influence or say does each of the following (superintendent, central office administrative staff, social work supervisor or immediate supervisor, and social worker) have on a decision about how the actual pattern of daily social services is carried out by the school social worker in your district?

Both of these questions are adapted from the work of Tannenbaum (1968) and Johnson (1978).

A rating of 1 (very little influence) to 5 (a very great influence) will be assigned to each position by the respondents. Scores for perceived centralization about program policy and perceived centralization about work will be arrived at by comparing the superintendent's rating to the aggregate ratings for all others (central office administrative staff, social work supervisor or immediate supervisor, and social worker). The ratio of superintendent's influence to the influence of all others for the question about job description will be the score for centralization about program policy. Similarly the ratio of superintendent's influence to the influence of all others for the question about daily social service delivery will be the score for centralization about work.

Formalization

Formalization refers to the extent of job codification in an organization and is defined as the degree to which rules govern daily work. A large amount of governance by rules means high formalization; a small amount of governance by rules means low formalization.

The indicator for formalization in this study will be a variation of Hall's job codification scale (1963). The scale will be administered as part of Instrument no. 1 and Instrument no. 2 (see Appendix A) to superintendents and supervisors and will measure perceived formalization of social work jobs. The degree of formalization will be determined by the question: How much is the daily practice of a school social worker determined by formal written rules and definitions of procedure in your district?

The scale ranges from 1 (very little) to 5 (a great deal). A high score means high formalization; a low score means low formalization.

Stratification

Stratification is the differential distribution of rewards in the organization and is measured in this study by a ratio of the salaries of the lowest and highest paid positions. A large difference in salaries means high stratification; a small difference in salaries means low stratification. This definition is similar to that employed by Snead (1967) in his test of the axiomatic theory. As part of Instrument no. 1 and Instrument no. 2 superintendents and supervisors are asked:

1. What is the annual salary (12 month) of the superintendent in your district?

2. What is the salary of an entry-level, B.A teacher in your district? Please state 9, 10, 11, 12 month or other basis of employment.

Utilization of a Research Recommendation

Utilization of a research recommendation means the degree to which the recommendation by Costin (1969a) is used by school districts. On mailed Instrument no. 3 (see Appendix A) mailed to social workers, two key questions will be asked. Each question will list eleven activities. The social workers will be asked how often each activity is performed in their school district (instrumental utilization) and if each activity is specifically identified in the operational description of school social work in the district (conceptual utilization). Perceived instrumental utilization will be measured by a Likert-type scale from 1 (very little) to 5 (a great deal). Perceived conceptual utilization will be measured by a 1 for a no response and a 2 for a yes response. Not sure responses are excluded from the statistical analysis. When more than one social worker in the district responds, the mean score on each item will be utilized. The questions are as follows:

1. How often are the following *activities performed* as part of the total school social work function in your school district over the normal academic year?
2. Are the following *activities specifically identified* in the operational description of school social work in your district?

Control Variables

District size, district resources, and district expenditures are the three control variables in the current study. District size is defined as student enrollment as of September 1, and superintendents were asked to provide this information on Instrument no. 1 (see Appendix A).

District resources is defined as the amount of money available to the district per pupil. District expenditures is defined as the amount of money spent by the district per pupil. Because each state uses different factors in computing per pupil resources and per pupil expenditures, ratings from 1 (low) to 4 (high) were assigned by the researcher within each state rather than for all states.

Ratings were assigned according to the following procedure for each state. The mean amount of resources per pupil and the mean amount of expenditures per pupil were obtained from information provided by each state office of education in its annual report. In the case of resources per pupil, the mean amount of resources per pupil was used as a base. Districts which had 25% *more* per pupil resources than the mean were assigned a 4. Districts which had the mean amount, or up to 24% *more* than the mean amount, were assigned a 3. Districts which had *less* than the mean amount, 99% to 75%, were assigned a 2. Districts with *less* than 25% of the mean resources were assigned a 1.

A similar rating procedure was used for district expenditures where ratings of 1 to 4 were also used. Appendix A provides complete details for each state in the category of resources and in the category of expenditures.

Table 5.1
Distribution of Sample

	TOTAL NUMBER OF DISTRICTS*	NUMBER IN SAMPLE	PERCENTAGE OF TOTAL NUMBER
New York	179	98	.55
North Carolina	115	63	.55
Connecticut	70	39	.55
	364	200	.55

Total districts reporting school social workers from lists obtained from state consultants for school social work.

POPULATION AND SAMPLE

The population consists of all public school districts which employ school social workers. The sample for this study is a purposive sample of public school districts in three states (New York, North Carolina, and Connecticut). The states have the following similar characteristics:

1. School social workers are certified by the state office of education.
2. There is a state consultant for school social work.
3. School social work has been in existence longer than fifteen years.
4. There is a state professional association of school social workers.

It is hoped, that by choosing states with these characteristics, the possible confounding effects of the current professional and legal status of school social work, prior school social work history, and access to Costin's research (1969a) will be limited. The school social workers in the sample use a variety of titles in additon to school social worker. These titles include visiting teacher, attendance officer, and home-school coordinator.

State consultants to school social work provided the universe of school district names and addresses in these three states. A random sample of 200 districts from the three states was proportionally stratified on the basis of the number of districts in each state.

Table 5.1 shows the distribution of school districts with social workers in each state and the size of the sample. In an attempt to control for extremes in the size

Table 5.2
Questionnaire Distribution

	NUMBER OF DISTRICTS	NUMBER OF SUPT.	NUMBER OF SUPER.	NUMBER OF S. W.
New York	98	98	98	174
North Carolina	63	63	63	112
Connecticut	39	39	39	93*
	200	200	200	379

Includes 10 social work coordinators or directors. SUPT. = Superintendent, SUPER. = Supervisor, S.W. = Social Worker.

of school districts and ensure the representativeness for the sample, school districts with more than 100,000 students were excluded because it was felt these districts would be atypical. Thus, the New York City Community District (enrollment exceeding 900,000) was excluded. All of the information about districts (district name, superintendent, address, size, and whether school social workers were employed) was obtained from the state consultant for school social work in each state.

Within the sample of districts, questionnaires were sent to each superintendent and the person designated as supervising school social workers. In addition, questionnaires were sent to each district's school social workers. Where there were one, two, or three social workers, each social worker was sent a questionnaire. In districts with more than three school social workers, a random sample of three social workers was sent questionnaires. If a person with the title "social work coordinator" or "director of social services" was identified as part of the social service unit, that person was also sent a social worker questionnaire.

A total of 779 questionnaires was sent to respondents in 200 school districts. The distribution of questionnaires is shown in Table 5.2.

INSTRUMENTS

Three self-report instruments were utilized to assess the relationship of organizational structure (complexity, centralization, formalization, and stratification) to the utilization of a research recommendation. These instruments were developed specifically for the present inquiry and guidelines for questionnaire construction were followed (Bradburn & Sudman 1980, Leedy 1980). A pretest was also conducted prior to the use of the final instruments.

Pretest

A pretest of the instruments, cover letters, and the procedures used was conducted in order to check for face validity and construct validity. Superintendents and social workers not in the sample were asked to respond to the clarity of the questions. Several rewordings followed.

School organizational charts were obtained from selected districts in order to compare perceived centralization with actual documentation. The social work job description and rule handbook of these districts were also obtained in order to compare perception with reality. There was agreement between perceived centralization and actual documentation and between perceived job codification and actual documents.

On the social worker instrument there was agreement between observed district utilization of Costin's recommendation and the self-report of utilization by its social workers. There was also internal consistency among individual social workers from the same district.

In addition to field-testing the instruments, the pretest consisted of an entry assessment and preliminary data reduction. Entry assessment was concerned with the problems of gaining people's interest and time to complete the questionnaire. Preliminary data reduction was done to see if there was sufficient variation in the responses to test the hypotheses and to see if the pretest findings appeared to have some validity.

The pretest revealed a possible entry problem of being able to obtain sufficient superintendent response. Many superintendents did not feel they had the time to respond to a mailed survey, and thus they either did not complete the questionnaire or asked an assistant superintendent or other central office administrator to complete it. It was decided to include a questionnaire to the person who supervises the social work staff, which would ask the same information as the superintendent's questionnaire. In most cases this was an assistant superintendent, although in some larger districts the supervisor was another central office administrator.

When the preliminary data were aggregated by hand tabulation, variation in responses for both the independent and dependent variables was evident. There were also some indicators that supported the hypotheses. This preliminary data reduction was also helpful in rearranging the format of the questions on the instrument and in developing the code book for the study.

Superintendent's Questionnaire

Instrument no. 1 is a brief, nine-item structured questionnaire (see Appendix A) for school superintendents, which focuses on obtaining information on complexity, centralization, formalization, and stratification. As previously discussed in the subsection on variables, Instrument no. 1 includes a centralization scale, a job codification scale, questions about the number of professionals and specialists employed by the district, and questions about the salaries of the superintendent and an entry-level teacher.

The instrument was accompanied by a cover letter explaining the importance of the study and requesting cooperation in completing the instrument. The letter delineated the purposes of the research and ensured anonymity for all participants. Copies of the results were offered to those interested and sufficient return postage was included.

Reliability on the perceived centralization scale was obtained by Tannenbaum (1968) by comparing two separate measures of control with the perceived centralization scale. He obtained correlation coefficients of .93 and .90. Face validity and construct validity were checked for in the pretest.

Reliability on the job codification scale was obtained by Hall (1963). Hall obtained split-half correlation coefficients ranging between .80 and .90. During the pretest, face validity and construct validity were checked by having superintendents not in the sample respond to the scale.

The questions about the number of professionals and specialists employed by the district and about the salaries of the superintendent and an entry-level teacher are factual. The accuracy of respondents' reporting was verified in the pretest sample. These questions are standard measures of complexity and stratification and are similar to Hage and Aiken's (1970) measures.

Supervisor's Questionnaire

Instrument no. 2 is the same nine-item structured questionnaire (see Appendix A) used for superintendents, except for its heading. It obtained information on the independent variables of complexity, centralization, formalization, and stratification. As discussed earlier, it was utilized because of problems during the pretest of getting sufficient superintendent response.

The supervisor's questionnaire along with a separate postage-paid return envelope was sent to the superintendent of each district because information about the supervisor's name and address was not available from directories. The letter to the superintendents requested them to personally complete the superintendent's questionnaire and to give the supervisor's questionnaire to the person who supervises school social workers in their district. This was done in order to ensure that data on the independent variables of complexity, centralization, formalization, and stratification could at least be obtained from an administrative position in each district if the superintendent did not complete his or her questionnaire. There was also the added advantage of comparing responses for consistency when both superintendent and supervisor returned the questionnaires.

School Social Worker's Questionnaire

Instrument no. 3 is a structured 22-item questionnaire for school social workers (see Appendix A). It was accompanied by a cover letter explaining the importance of the study and requesting cooperation in completing the instrument. It offered a copy of the results and ensured anonymity for all participants. Return postage was also included.

The major focus of the questionnaire was to determine instrumental and conceptual utilization of Costin's research recommendation (1969a). This was done by breaking Costin's recommendation (see Chapter 4) down into its specific components (consultation with school administrators in formulation of administrative policy, consultation with teachers on general classroom issues, group work with students, work with parents on students' rights issues, and assistance in resource development and planned change in the community). These components were then mixed with traditional casework activities (direct services to individual students, direct services to families, consultation with teachers on individual students, interpretation of school social work services, and liaison between the family and the community). In addition, the social case history was included as an activity after the pretest when a number of social workers reported that they spent a great deal of time preparing social histories since P.L. 94-142.

As discussed earlier in the section on variables, social workers were asked to rate each of these eleven activities from very little (1) to a great deal (5) in relation to the question for instrumental utilization. For the question on conceptual utilization, the responses were no, yes, or not sure, with no receiving a score of 1 and yes receiving a score of 2. Not sure responses were excluded from statistical analysis.

For comparison, but not as a major focus of the study, the instrument also asks how often the school social worker personally performs the eleven activities. The organization is the unit of analysis in the study, and thus this data is for informational purposes only.

Also for informational purposes only, a brief description of Costin's study (1969a) is given and respondents are asked if they have heard of Professor Costin's recommendation and how and when they heard of it. If they have heard of the recommendation, they will also be asked how much the recommendation has influenced both the organization's ideas and activities about school social work and their personal ideas and activities about school social work. The question is: How much has the recommendation in Professor Costin's article influenced:

(a) specific programs and activities of your district's social work unit;
(b) thinking and ideas about school social work practice in your district's social work unit;
(c) the pattern of your personal school social work professional practice;
(d) your personal thinking and ideas about school social work?

Several other open-ended questions are also included on the instrument but these are not the major focus of the study. These concern the impact of P.L. 94-142, federal budget cuts, desegregation, and the age of the social work

Table 5.3
Completed Questionnaires*

	NUMBER OF DISTRICTS**	NUMBER OF SUPT.	NUMBER OF SUPER.	NUMBER OF S.W.
New York	81 (83)	61 (61)	40 (41)	92 (53)
North Carolina	55 (87)	43 (68)	27 (43)	41 (37)
Connecticut	39 (100)	31 (79)	18 (46)	53 (57)
	175 (88)	135 (68)	85 (43)	186 (49)

Numbers in parentheses are the percentage of completed questionnaires.
**A district was counted if there was any response from superintendent, supervisor, or social worker.
SUPT. = Superintendent, SUPER. = Supervisor, S.W. = Social Worker.

program in their school district. In addition, the questions on complexity, centralization, formalization, and stratification (the independent variable) which were asked of the superintendent and supervisor are included in the social work questionnaire as a cross-check for consistency and also as a possible source of information when the superintendent and supervisor do not return their questionnaires.

PROCEDURES FOR DATA COLLECTION

Directories of school districts and school social workers were obtained from the state consultants for school social work and the proportionally stratified random sample of 200 districts was chosen. The cover letters and instruments were pretested and then were revised and prepared in final form. Following the sample selection and pretest, the letters and instruments were mailed to superintendents and social workers of each district. Supervisor's questionnaires were included with the superintendent's questionnaires as explained earlier in the instrument section. Postage-paid return envelopes were included for all respondents.

After three weeks, responses were received from 102 districts. Then duplicate questionnaires were mailed to nonrespondents. After a total time of six weeks, responses were received from 175 districts. The distribution of responses is shown in Table 5.3.

Contrary to the pretest, there was a good response from superintendents. The superintendents' response rate (68%) was higher than the social workers' response rate (49%) or the supervisors' response rate (43%).

Table 5.4
Nonrespondent Districts*

REASON	NUMBER	PERCENT
No social worker currently	11	5.5
Unknown reason, no return	10	5.0
Incorrect address, not forwardable	2	1.0
Did not wish to participate	2	1.0
TOTAL	25	12.5

Total number of districts in sample is 200.

Although bias could result from systematic differences between districts with responses and districts without responses, it is felt that having 88% of the districts with a response (either social worker, supervisor, or superintendent) is a reasonable basis for a valid analysis and justifies using only completed returns.

Also an examination of the 12.5% of the districts from which no response was received revealed no consistent pattern. Several of the districts that had no social workers returned their questionnaires with that fact written on the top of the questionnaire. Due to changing school district budgets, it is very probable that other districts were no longer able to employ social workers and simply failed to return their questionnaires. The breakdown on nonrespondents is provided in Table 5.4.

Since the organization is the unit of analysis, only districts which contained matched responses were used in the final analysis. A matched response is where at least one social worker's response and the superintendent's response were returned. The use of matched districts was essential in order to examine the relationship between utilization responses reported by social workers and organizational structure responses reported by superintendents. It is not likely that an analysis that includes 51% of the sample will detract sufficiently from the results; however, caution needs to be taken in generalizing from the results. The distribution of matched districts and the percentage of sample is shown in Table 5.5.

PROCEDURES FOR DATA CODING AND ANALYSIS

Responses to the questionnaires were coded and keypunched on computer cards and then transferred to a permanent file tape to facilitate analysis. The

Table 5.5
Matched Districts*

	NUMBER OF DISTRICTS	PERCENT OF SAMPLE	PERCENT OF RETURNED SAMPLE
New York	50	51%	67%
North Carolina	26	41%	47%
Connecticut	26	67%	67%
	102	51%	58%

A matched district is a district where a superintendent and social work response were received.

Statistical Package for the Social Sciences (SPSS) system of computer programs, designed for the analysis of social science data, was utilized in this research. Data processing was conducted at the University of Texas Computation Center at Austin, Texas. Hypothesized relationships between variables were tested using Pearson's product-moment correlation coefficients. Multiple linear regression was used to examine the relationships of all the independent variables and utilization of Costin's research recommendation. T-tests were used to see if there were any significant differences between high-users and low-users of Costin's research recommendation.

6 Characteristics of the Sample

This chapter provides an overview of the characteristics of the sample. The univariate frequency distributions for all variables in the study are reported. The chapter summarizes the characteristics of the sample for district complexity, centralization, formalization, stratification, utilization of Costin's research recommendation, size, resources, and expenditures. The measure of central tendency and measure of variability are also provided for each variable.

Because measures of central tendency make it possible to describe the location of a distribution of values with a single number, each variable's mean will be reported. In instances where a variable is composed of data from responses to several questions, the mean response for each subquestion will also be reported. The variation will be described by reporting the standard deviation or the extent to which the values vary from the mean. When relevant, the range of responses will also be discussed.

Complexity

As discussed earlier, complexity in this study is defined as the ratio of specialized personnel to other professional school personnel. The ratio was determined from responses to two questions to the superintendents on Instrument no. 1. The distribution of responses appears in Table 6.1.

The immediate implication when a standard deviation is larger than the mean is that the distribution is skewed, and this is the case for the present sample. Despite the large range in the number of total professionals, over 70% of the districts had 400 or fewer total professionals and only 4% of the districts had 1,000 or more total professionals. The median number of professionals was 299. Similarly, in the category of other professionals, 71% of the districts had 50 or fewer professionals and less than 8% of the districts had more than 100 other professionals. The median number of other professionals was 36.

Table 6.1
Number of Professionals

QUESTION	MEAN	STANDARD DEVIATION	RANGE	NUMBER OF CASES
4. What is the total number of certified professionals (employees with a B.A. or more) currently employed by your district?	401	463	3267	135
5. How many of the above certified professionals have job titles other than classroom teacher?	52	57	399	135

The responses from the questions on number of professionals were put into ratio form to determine the degree of district complexity, i.e., the number of certified professionals with job titles other than classroom teacher compared to the total number of certified professionals. The mean response for degree of job complexity was 0.1357, or 13.57%, and the standard deviation was 0.0587. The range for degree of job complexity was 0.3018. In practical terms, the degree of job complexity (0.1357) means that about 13% of the professional staff consists of specialized personnel other than teachers in this sample.

Centralization

Centralization in this study is defined as the degree of influence that the superintendent, the highest organizational position, has in decision making. Two kinds of decision making are considered in this study: decision making about program policy (question no. 1 from Instrument no. 1) and decision-making about work (question no. 2 from Instrument no. 1). A rating of 1 (very little influence) to 5 (a very great influence) was assigned to each position (superintendent, central administration, social work supervisor, and social worker) by the respondents. The responses are reported in Table 6.2.

Centralization about program policy was determined by comparing the superintendent's rating of influence to the aggregate rating of influence for all others for question no. 1. The category of all others includes the central administration, social work supervisor, and social worker positions. The ratio of superintendent's influence to the aggregate of the influence of all others is the score for centralization about policy. In this sample, the mean score for centralization

Table 6.2
Influence Ratings*

QUESTION	POSITION	MEAN	STANDARD DEVIATION	NUMBER OF CASES
1. How much influence or say does each of the following have on a decision about the content of the job description of the school social worker in your district?	Superintendent	3.726	1.432	135
	Central Administration	3.291	1.408	134
	Social Work Supervisor	4.261	.901	134
	Social Worker	3.667	1.216	135
2. How much influence or say does each of the following have on a decision about how the actual pattern of daily activities is carried out by the school social worker in your district?	Superintendent	2.178	1.292	135
	Central Administration	2.386	1.334	132
	Social Work Supervisor	4.133	1.035	135
	Social Worker	4.363	.886	135

*1 = Very Little, 2 = Some, 3 = A Fair Amount, 4 = A Good Deal, 5 = A Great Deal

Table 6.3
Rule Governance*

QUESTION*	MEAN	STANDARD DEVIATION	NUMBER OF CASES
3. How much is the daily practice of a school social worker determined by formal written rules and definitions of procedures in your district?	2.8284	1.4381	134

1 = Very Little, 2 = Some, 3 = A Fair Amount, 4 = A Good Deal, 5 = A Great Deal

about program policy is 3.578 with a standard deviation of 0.2027, using 134 cases.

Centralization about work was determined by comparing the superintendent's rating of influence to the aggregate rating of influence for all others for question no. 2. The category of all others again includes the central administration, social work supervisor, and social worker. The ratio of superintendent's influence to the aggregate of the influence of all others is the score for centralization about work. In the current study the mean score for centralization about work is 2.035, with a standard deviation of .1308, using 132 cases.

The mean score for centralization about program policy is thus higher than the mean score for centralization about work. The practical implications of this are that, in general, school district superintendents were perceived to have more influence in decisions about job descriptions of social workers than in decisions about the daily activities of social workers. This finding also supports the face validity of the study since this result would be expected.

Formalization

Formalization in this study is defined as the degree to which rules govern the daily work of the school social worker. The degree of formalization is determined by responses to question no. 3 on Instrument no. 1 to superintendents. Responses range from 1 (very little) to 5 (a great deal). Table 6.3 shows the distribution of responses.

In practical terms, this table means that the average district is perceived to govern a fair amount of the practice of school social work by rules. This result again supports the face validity of the study, since it would be expected that the

Table 6.4
Monthly Salary

QUESTION	MEAN	STANDARD DEVIATION	RANGE	NUMBER OF CASES
6. What is the annual salary (12 mo.) of the superintendent in your district?*	$3911.54	$775.26	$3233	135
7. What is the salary of an entry-level, B.A. teacher in your district? Please state 9, 10, 11, 12 mo. or other basis of employment.*	$1321.54	$143.20	$850	135

Annual salaries were converted to monthly salaries for standardization of the results. A 12 month basis is shown for all districts.

mean response would reflect a middle range of rule governance and not either of the extremes of a very little or a great deal.

Stratification

In the current study, stratification is defined as the differential distribution of rewards in the organization, and the degree of stratification is measured by the difference in salaries between the superintendent and an entry-level teacher. Responses to question no. 6 and question no. 7 on Instrument no. 1 are shown in Table 6.4. Since salaries were reported on other than an annual basis in some cases, salary responses were standardized by converting them to monthly salaries. This conversion was done by the researcher in order to facilitate the analysis of the data.

The difference in salaries was determined by a ratio of entry-level teacher's salary to superintendent's salary. The mean stratification score was 0.3489 with a standard deviation of 0.0587, using 135 cases. In practical terms, this finding means that entry-level teachers earned about 35% of a superintendent's salary for this sample.

Utilization of Costin's
Research Recommendation

Utilization of Costin's research recommendation was defined in two parts for this study. Instrumental utilization of the research recommendation was defined

Table 6.5
Performance of Costin's Activities

QUESTION*	MEAN	STANDARD DEVIATION	NUMBER OF CASES
la. Students' Rights	2.099	1.151	140
lb. Group Work	2.745	1.3	140
lf. General Consultation	2.43	1.195	140
lg. Res. Devel./Com. Change	2.278	1.103	140
lj. Admin. Consultation	2.426	1.260	140
Five Costin Activities	2.392	.912	140
Six Traditional Activities	3.782	.631	140
All Activities	3.15	.581	140

*See full question in Appendix A.

1 = Very Little, 2 = Some, 3 = A Fair Amount, 4 = A Good Deal, 5 = A Great Deal

as the degree to which the recommendation was used by school districts in a documentable way (performance of daily activities). Conceptual utilization was defined as the degree to which Costin's recommendation influenced thinking (identification of activities in job description).

Question no. 1 on Instrument no. 3 listed eleven activities, which social workers were to rate on a scale of 1 (very little) to 5 (a great deal) in relation to how often each activity was performed in their school district. The mean of the ratings of the five Costin recommended activities of question no. 1 was the instrumental utilization score. Table 6.5 reports the results.

It is evident that group work was reported to be performed most often and student rights was reported to be performed least often. The mean score for instrumental utilization (Costin's five recommended activities) is, however, less than the mean score for performance of all eleven activities and the six traditional activities. This means that the five Costin-recommended activities on the whole

Table 6.6
Identification of Costin's Activities

QUESTION*	MEAN	STANDARD DEVIATION	NUMBER OF CASES
2a. Students' Rights	1.33	.442	117
2b. Group Work	1.703	.439	127
2f. General Consultation	1.593	.466	122
2g. Res. Devel./Com. Change	1.493	.473	121
2j. Admin. Consultation	1.517	.477	119
Five Costin Activities	1.550	.325	135
Six Traditional Activities	1.929	.119	135
All Activities	1.761	.177	135

See full question in Appendix A.
1 = No, 2 = Yes

were performed less than the other general social work activities. The six traditional activities were, as expected, performed the most often.

Question no. 2 on Instrument no. 3 again listed eleven activities to which social workers were to assign a no (1) or yes (2) response as to whether the activity was specifically identified in the job description of the school social worker of their district. The mean of the five Costin recommended activities, or question no. 2, was the conceptual utilization score. Table 6.6 describes the results. Again, group work was most often included in job descriptions and students' rights was least often included. Costin's recommended activities are reported to appear less frequently in job descriptions than the six traditional activities or all eleven activities. The six traditional activities have the highest mean and were included in almost every district's job description. This result was expected and supports the face validity of the question.

Size, Resources, and Expenditures

District size, district resources, and district expenditures were the control variables utilized in the study. The information on size was reported on Instrument

Table 6.7
District Size, District Resources, and District Expenditures

CONTROL VARIABLE	MEAN	STANDARD DEVIATION	RANGE	NUMBER OF CASES
Size	6172	7371	53358	135
Resources*	2.496	1.007	3.0	135
Expenditures*	2.533	.983	3.0	135

The means for district resources and expenditures were determined from a ranking within each state of 1 (low) to 4 (high). See Chapter 5 and Appendix A for a complete discussion of the procedure.

no. 1 by the superintendent and the information on district resources and district expenditures was obtained from documents provided by state offices of education. Table 6.7 summarizes the results.

Because the standard deviation is larger than the mean, it is evident that the distribution of size in this sample is skewed. In fact, there is a range of 53,358 students. Additional examination of the results reveals that the median size of the districts in the sample is 4,400 students and the mode is 5,000 students. Since the results for resources and expenditures are means determined from rank orders of only 1 to 4, a middle range response was expected.

PART III

PRESENT AND
FUTURE IMPLICATIONS

7 Results

This chapter presents the results of the analysis of the data. This analysis examines the central problem of the study, the relationship between organizational structure and the utilization of Costin's research recommendation. As discussed in Chapter 5, the primary analysis of the data will include only matched responses from the superintendents' questionnaires (Instrument no. 1) and the social workers' questionnaires (Instrument no. 3). Data from the supervisors' questionnaires (Instrument no. 2) will be discussed in the section "Other Analyses," where secondary analyses of the data are presented. It is important to note again that in this study the organization is the unit of analysis and responses are thus aggregated by school districts and not by individuals.

The chapter is subdivided into four sections in order to facilitate the presentation of the results. The first three sections deal directly with the primary analysis, and the fourth section is a summary of the other relevant but secondary analyses.

The first section discusses the results of a simple correlational analysis of each organizational structure variable and utilization of Costin's research recommendation. The hypothesized relationships between the independent variables (complexity, centralization, formalization, and stratification) and the dependent variable (utilization of Costin's research recommendation) are considered.

The second section presents the results of partial correlational analysis in order to determine the relationship between the organizational structure variables and utilization of Costin's research recommendation when controlling for district size, resources, and expenditures. First-order and third-order relationships are described.

The third section shows the results of multiple linear regression analyses. All of the independent variables were included together in the equation in order to see how much these organizational structure variables can predict the dependent variable (utilization of Costin's research recommendation).

The fourth section presents the results of other analyses which are relevant to the study but of secondary importance. These include the use of different respondents, item analyses, supplemental questions, comparison of results with traditional activities and all activities, and regrouping the sample.

PEARSON PRODUCT-MOMENT CORRELATIONS

The Pearson *r* is a measure of relationship for interval variables that shows the strength and direction of a relationship. First, the bivariate relationship between each variable in the study is examined, and then the hypothesized relationships are discussed.

All Variables

When all bivariate relationships were examined, a two-tailed test of significance was employed. In addition, cases with missing data were deleted. Table 7.1 shows the results.

If one looks at the strongest correlations first, it is obvious that they occur when the researcher divided one variable into two components. For example, district wealth was divided into district resources and district expenditures, and these two separate variables have a correlation over 0.76. Similarly centralization was divided into centralization about policy and centralization about work, and the separate variables correlate above 0.59. The same is true for utilization, which was divided into instrumental and conceptual utilization, with the separate variables correlating above 0.48. The other strong correlation, the relationship between formalization and instrumental utilization (with a correlation above .57) was predicted in the hypotheses and will be discussed in the next section on hypothesized relationships.

Several of the other weaker correlations are in accord with Hage's axiomatic theory discussed in Chapter 3. For instance, complexity and centralization about work ($r = -0.18$) follows Proposition VII, centralization about policy and formalization ($r = 0.25$) follows Proposition III, centralization about work and formalization ($r = 0.28$) follows Proposition III, and centralization about work and stratification follows Corollary 19.

Other significant but weak correlations are the relationships involving the control variables of district size, district resources, and district expenditures. Centralization about work was negatively related to expenditures with the implication that highly centralized districts spend less than districts where decision-making power is less centralized. Formalization was positively related to size, which suggests that large districts are governed more by rules than small districts. Stratification was negatively related to size, resources, and expenditures. The implication is that there is a greater difference between the superintendent's salary and an entry-level teacher's salary in smaller and poorer districts. Further examination reveals that the smaller and poorer districts have a lower entry-level teacher's salary than the larger and wealthier districts.

Table 7.1
Pearson Product-Moment Correlations for all Variables

	COMP	CAP	CAW	FORM	STRAT	SIZE	RES	EXP	IU	CU
Independent Variables										
Comp	1.0									
CAP	-.1321 (132) P=.128	1.0								
CAW	-.1832 (130) P=.036	.5909 (129) P=.001	1.0							
Form	-.1223 (132) P=.159	.2460 (131) P=.004	.2814 (129) P=.001	1.0						
Strat	-.1193 (133) P=.168	.0723 (132) P=.406	.1742 (130) P=.046	-.1175 (132) P=.176	1.0					

Table 7.1 (continued)

Control Variables

	C1	C2	C3	C4	C5	C6	C7	C8	C9	C10
Size -	.1183 (133) P=.172	-.1204 (132) P=.166	-.0099 (130) P=.910	.2533 (132) P=.003	-.2171 (133) P=.011	1.0				
Res	.1355 (133) P=.117	-.1096 (132) P=.207	-.1306 (130) P=.136	-.0487 (130) P=.576	-.2426 (133) P=.005	-.0781 (133) P=.368	1.0			
Exp	.0314 (139) P=.129	-.1449 (132) P=.095	-.1878 (130) P=.031	.0135 (132) P=.877	-.4646 (133) P=.001	-.353 (133) P=.685	.7635 (133) P=.001	1.0		

Dependent Variables

	C1	C2	C3	C4	C5	C6	C7	C8	C9	C10
IU	.0871 (101) P=.382	-.3378 (100) P=.001	-.2945 (99) P=.003	-.5734 (100) P=.001	.1017 (100) P=.307	-.1403 (101) P=.157	.0795 (101) P=.425	-.0024 (101) P=.981	1.0	
CU	.1295 (98) P=.199	-.1150 (97) P=.257	-.0804 (96) P=.431	-.2235 (97) P=.026	.1345 (98) P=.182	-.0640 (98) P=.527	.0743 (98) P=.463	.0551 (98) P=.586	.4845 (133) P=.001	1.0

*P is significance level and the number in parentheses is the number of cases. When the significance level is set at .05 or less for these 45 relationships, one would expect 2 significant relationships to occur by chance alone. The results show that 16 significant relationships occur. This finding suggests that it is likely the significant relationships did not occur by chance.

Hypothesized Relationships

By using the two-tailed test of significance, as shown in Table 7.1, the direction of all the relationships hypothesized in Chapter 5 was found to be consistent with the hypotheses with the exception of the relationship between stratification and utilization of Costin's recommendation. However, only four relationships were significant at the .05 level or above. These were the relationships between centralization about policy and instrumental utilization, between centralization about work and instrumental utilization, between formalization and instrumental utilization, and between formalization and conceptual utilization.

The relationship between formalization and instrumental utilization ($r = -0.57$) can be considered a moderate relationship while the relationship between centralization about policy and instrumental utilization ($r = -0.34$). centralization about work and instrumental utilization ($r = -0.29$), and formalization and conceptual utilization ($r = -0.22$) can be considered low.

Formalization is the only organizational structure variable that correlates significantly with both instrumental and conceptual utilization. This finding suggests that it may be the most important of the organizational structure variables considered in this study.

By using a one-tailed test of significance for the hypothesized relationships, which can be justified because of the theoretical support for the study's hypotheses, the significance of the relationships between centralization about work and instrumental utilization and between formalization and conceptual utilization are higher. Table 7.2 shows the hypothesized relationships using a one-tailed test of significance.

PARTIAL CORRELATIONS

District size, district resources, and district expenditures were included in this study as possible control variables. First- and third-order partial correlations were done with cases with missing data deleted. The results are shown in Table 7.3 and Table 7.4.

The relationships between the independent and dependent variables are not greatly affected by the control variables. A comparison of the results shows that size has the most effect. The net change in the relationship between centralization about policy and instrumental utilization is -0.023 when size is controlled and is -0.0265 when size, resources, and expenditures are simultaneously controlled. The net change in the relationship between formalization and instrumental utilization is 0.0118 when size is controlled and is 0.0135 when size, resources, and expenditures are simultaneously controlled. District resources and expenditures have very little effect on the relationships between the organizational structure variables and the utilization of Costin's research recommendation.

Table 7.2
Pearson Product-Moment Correlations for Hypothesized Variables* (Using One-Tailed Test)

	COMPLEXITY	CENTRALIZATION ABOUT POLICY	CENTRALIZATION ABOUT WORK	FORMALIZATION	STRATIFICATION
Instrumental Utilization	.0871 (102) P=.191	-.3378 (102) **P=.001	-.2945 (101) **P=.001	-.5731 (102) **P=.001	.1017 (102) P=.153
Conceptual Utilization	.1295 (100) P=.100	-.1150 (99) P=.129	.0804 (98) P=.216	-.2232 (99) **P=.013	-.1345 (100) P=.091

*P is significance level and the number in parentheses is the number of cases.

**Significant at .05 level.

82

Table 7.3
First-Order Relationships*

	COMPLEXITY	CENTRALIZATION ABOUT POLICY	CENTRALIZATION ABOUT WORK	FORMALIZATION	STRATIFICATION
Controlling for Size					
Instrumental Utilization	.0717 (100) P=.474	-.3608 (99) P=.001	-.2989 (98) P=.003	-.5616 (99) P=.001	.0737 (100) P=.462
Conceptual Utilization	.1230 (97) P=.225	-.1238 (96) P=.224	-.0812 (95) P=.429	-.2147 (96) P=.034	.1238 (97) P=-.222
Controlling for Resources					
Instrumental Utilization	.0772 (100) P=.440	-.3321 (99) P=.001	.2875 (98) P=.004	-.5720 (99) P=.001	.1251 (100) P=.210
Conceptual Utilization	.1230 (97) P=.233	-.1238 (96) P=.291	-.0812 (95) P=.486	-.2147 (96) P=.029	.1238 (97) P=.119
Controlling for Expenditures					
Instrumental Utilization	.0881 (100) P=.378	-.3417 (99) P=.001	-.3003 (98) P=.002	-.5734 (99) P=.001	.1136 (100) P=.256
Conceptual Utilization	.1235 (97) P=.323	.1086 (96) P=.289	-.0714 (95) P=.487	-.2246 (96) P=.026	.1810 (97) P=.073

*P is significance level and the number in parentheses is the number of cases.

Table 7.4
Third-Order Relationships* Controlling for Size, Resources, and Expenditures

	COMPLEXITY	CENTRALIZATION ABOUT POLICY	CENTRALIZATION ABOUT WORK	FORMALIZATION	STRATIFICATION
Instrumental Utilization	.0687 (98) P=.497	-.3643 (97) **P=.002	-.3076 (96) **P=.002	-.5599 (97) **P=.001	.0687 (98) P=.497
Conceptual Utilization	.1152 (95) P=.261	-.1164 (94) P=.259	-.0727 (93) P=.484	-.2137 (94) *P=.037	.1667 (95) P=.103

*P is significance level and the number in parentheses is the number of cases.

**Significant at .05 level

Table 7.5
Regression Analysis for Instrumental Utilization

STEP	VARIABLE ENTERED	R^2	R^2 CHANGE	F RATIO	P
1	Formalization	.32882	.32882	26.94465	.000
2	Centralization about Policy	.37000	.04118	15.85706	.000
3	Stratification	.37315	.00316	10.51679	.000
4	Resources	.37530	.00214	7.80991	.000
5	Expenditures	.37819	.00289	6.20363	.000
6	Centralization about Work	.38000	.00181	5.10751	.000
7	Size	.38024	.00024	4.29463	.001

REGRESSION ANALYSES

In order to examine further the relationship of organizational structure variables to the utilization of Costin's research recommendation, multiple linear regression analyses were employed. For both instrumental utilization and conceptual utilization, the independent variables (complexity, centralization about policy, centralization about work, formalization, and stratification) and the control variables (size, resources, and expenditures) were entered into the equation. Cases with missing data were deleted.

The multiple linear regression analysis for instrumental utilization is presented in Table 7.5, and although not significant at the 0.05 level, the multiple linear regression analysis for conceptual utilization is presented in Table 7.6.

For instrumental utilization, the change in the R^2 is seen to be largely concentrated in formalization (R^2 change $= 0.328$) and in centralization about policy (R^2 change $= 0.041$). No other variables are associated with notatable change in R^2. Formalization and centralization about policy account for over 36% of the variance in instrumental utilization. The total contribution of all the variables explained 38% of the variance in instrumental utilization of Costin's research recommendation. The implication is that the organizational structure variables of formalization and centralization about policy are important predictors of the utilization of Costin's recommendation.

For conceptual utilization, the results are not significant at the 0.05 level, but

Table 7.6
Regression Analysis for Conceptual Utilization

STEP	VARIABLE ENTERED	R^2	R^2 CHANGE	F RATIO	P
1	Formalization	.04996	.04996	2.89204	.095
2	Stratification	.06183	.01187	1.77937	.178
3	Expenditures	.07699	.01517	1.47369	.232
4	Complexity	.08891	.01192	1.26870	.294
5	Centralization about Policy	.09147	.00256	1.02696	.412
6	Size	.09212	.00065	.84554	.541

if one uses a higher level such as 0.10, the largest change in R^2 is found again in formalization (R^2 change = 0.05). No other variables are significant, even at this higher level of significance.

OTHER ANALYSES

Although not of primary importance to the objectives of the study, several other secondary analyses are relevant. These include using different respondents, analyzing individual items in questions, asking supplemental questions, comparing Costin's activities with traditional activities, comparing Costin's activities with all activities, and regrouping the sample.

Different Respondents

Social workers, superintendents, and supervisors were all asked for information about the variables or centralization about policy, centralization about work, and formalization. A comparison of the mean responses of each group of respondents is shown in Table 7.7.

It is evident that very little difference was obtained in the mean responses. Supervisors and superintendents differed a little in their responses on formalization and centralization about policy but were exactly the same on centralization about work. Also social workers did perceive their school districts to be slightly more rule-oriented and less centralized than superintendents or supervisors did. It is also true that, for this sample, centralization about work was perceived to be less than centralization about policy. The implication is that, for this sample,

Table 7.7
Different Respondents

VARIABLE	POSITION	MEAN	STANDARD DEVIATION	NUMBER OF CASES
Formalization	Supt.	2.828	1.438	134
Formalization	Super.	3.012	1.210	85
Formalization	S.W.	3.018	1.337	139
Centralization about Policy	Supt.	.358	.203	134
Centralization about Policy	Super.	.322	.153	81
Centralization about Policy	S.W.	.312	.196	135
Centralization about Work	Supt.	.204	.131	132
Centralization about Work	Super.	.204	.128	80
Centralization about Work	S. W.	.192	.161	135

Supt. = Superintendent, Super. = Supervisor, S.W. = Social Worker.

respondents believed that social workers had more influence in decisions about their daily activities than they did in decisions about their job description. This finding would be expected and thus again supports the face validity of the questions about centralization.

Table 7.8 presents a correlational analysis of the different respondents. Again, it is evident that the superintendents and supervisors responded similarly on the questions about formalization ($r = 0.56$), on the question about centralization about policy ($r = 0.44$), and on the question about centralization about work ($r = 0.43$). Social workers' responses did not correlate very highly with superintendents' responses on the question about centralization about policy ($r = 0.19$) or on the question about centralization about work ($r = 0.14$).

Regression analyses were also done using the supervisors' responses and the

Table 7.8
Correlations of Different Respondents*

	SUPT.	SUPER.	S.W.
Formalization			
Supt.	1.0	.5636 (79) P=.001	.4937 (79) P=.001
Super.	.5632 (79) P=.001	1.0	.2973 (59) P=.02
S.W.	.4937 (79) P=.001	.2973 (59) P=.02	1.0
Centralization about Policy			
Supt.	1.0	.4441 (75) P=.001	.1876 (97) P=.063
Super.	.4441 (75) P=.001	1.0	.4839 (56) P=.001
S. W.	.1876 (97) P=.063	.4839 (56) P=.001	1.0
Centralization about Work			
Supt.	1.0	.4263 (72) P=.001	.1428 (96) P=.161
Super.	.4263 (72) P=.001	1.0	.4826 (55) P=.001
S. W.	.1428 (96) P=.161	.4826 (55) P=.001	1.0

P is significance level and the number in parentheses is the number of cases. Supt. = Superintendent, Super. = Supervisor, S. W. = Social Worker.

social workers' responses. For instrumental utilization, using the supervisors' responses rather than the superintendents' responses resulted in 18% of the variance being explained by formalization and centralization about policy. For instrumental utilization, using the social workers' responses resulted in 33% of the variable being explained by formalization. For conceptual utilization, the regression analyses were not significant for either supervisors' responses or social workers' responses. The implication of these secondary analyses is that formalization remains as the most important organizational structure variable and that it is a better predictor for instrumental utilization than conceptual utilization despite which responses are used in the analysis. The discrepancy in results when different respondents are used, however, suggests the need for further investigation of different perceptions of organizational structure.

Item Analyses for Individual Questions

An analysis of how individual items in question no. 1 and question no. 2 on the social worker's questionnaire (Instrument no. 3) correlated with the variables in the study was also done. A two-tailed test of significance was used and the significance level was set at .05 or less. Cases with missing data were deleted. Table 7.9 shows moderate to high correlations between the individual items of question no. 1 (students' rights, group work, general consultation, resource development, community change, administrative consultation) and instrumental utilization. This result was expected, since the mean of these individual items was used to determine instrumental utilization. Administrative consultation had the strongest correlation to instrumental utilization with $r = 0.81$. The individual items also correlate significantly with the organizational structure variables of centralization about policy, centralization about work, and formalization.

Correlations were not as high between the individual items of question no. 2 and the variables. There were moderate correlations between the individual items of question no. 2 (students' rights, group work, general consultation, resource development/community change, administrative consultation) and conceptual utilization. This result was expected because the mean of these individual items is the score for conceptual utilization. Administrative consultation had the highest correlation with conceptual utilization, with $r = 0.74$. As far as correlations with organizational structure variables, only resource development/community change correlated with centralization about policy and with formalization, and administrative consultation correlated with stratification. The other correlations between individual items on question no. 2 and the variables were not significant. The implication here is that administrative consultation is strongly related to conceptual utilization. Also only one item (resource development/community change) of the five items in question no. 2 correlated with formalization even though the mean of all the items as a whole correlated with formalization. This result suggests that the relationship of formalization to conceptual research utilization must be considered very weak at the most.

Table 7.9
The Relationship of Individual Items in the Research Utilization Questions to the Major Variables*

QUESTION #1	IU	CU	COMP	CAP	CAW	FORM	STRAT
1a. Students' Rights	.7133 (140) P=.001	.3160 (135) P=.001	.0111 (102) P=.912	-.3218 (102) P=.001	-.1160 (101) P=.248	-.4378 (102) P=.001	.1699 (103) P=.086
1b. Group Work	.7287 (139) P=.001	.3780 (134) P=.001	.1127 (102) P=.259	-.2197 (101) P=.027	-.1622 (100) P=.107	-.3625 (101) P=.001	.0198 (102) P=.843
1f. General Consultation	.7742 (140) P=.001	.4073 (135) P=.001	.0549 (102) P=.582	-.1963 (102) P=.048	-.1884 (101) P=.059	-.3028 (102) P=.002	.0575 (102) P=.564
1g. Res. Develop./ Com. Change	.7663 (139) P=.001	.3202 (134) P=.001	-.0010 (102) P=.992	-.2454 (102) P=.013	-.2833 (101) P=.004	-.4741 (102) P=.001	.0533 (102) P=.593
1j. Administrative	.8052 (140) P=.001	.4001 (135) P=.001	.1389 (102) P=.162	-.3257 (102) P=.002	-.3827 (101) P=.001	-.6107 (102) P=.001	.1019 (102) P=.306

Table 7.9 (continued)

QUESTION #2

		IU	CU	COMP	CAP	CAW	FORM	Strat
2a.	Students' Rights	.3789 (117) P=.001	.6400 (117) P=.001	.1865 (89) P=.08	-.1561 (88) P=.147	-.1916 (87) P=.075	-.1067 (88) P=.322	.1731 (89) P=.105
2b.	Group Work	.2340 (127) P=.008	.5951 (127) P=.001	.0268 (95) P=.796	-.0072 (94) P=.945	-.0815 (93) P=.437	-.1547 (94) P=.137	.1015 (95) P=.328
2f.	General Consultation	.4079 (122) P=.001	.7241 (122) P=.001	.0856 (90) P=.423	-.0196 (98) P=.855	-.0373 (88) P=.730	-.1780 (89) P=.095	.0578 (90) P=.589
2g.	Res. Develop./ Com. Change	.4477 (121) P=.001	.7042 (121) P=.001	.1161 (88) P=.281	-.2454 (87) P=.022	-.1193 (86) P=.274	-.2698 (89) P=.001	.1185 (88) P=.272
2j.	Administrative Consultation	.3308 (119) P=.001	.7393 (119) P=.001	.0700 (91) P=.510	-.0800 (90) P=.454	-.1044 (89) P=.330	-.1806 (90) P=.089	.2291 (91) P=.029

*P is significance level and the number in parentheses is the number of cases. IU = Instrumental Utilization, CU = Conceptual Utilization, COMP = Complexity, CAP = Centralization about Policy, CAW = Centralization about Work, FORM = Formalization, Strat = Stratification

Table 7.10

Regression Analysis Results for Items in Instrumental Utilization Question

QUESTION*	R^2	P
1a. Students' Rights	.30479	.000
1b. Group Work	.18427	.014
1f. General Consultation	.11862	.103
1g. Res. Development, Com. Change	.29428	.000
1j. Administrative Consultation	.42911	.000

Full questions are provided in Appendix A.

Regression analyses were also done between the organizational structure variables and the individual items in questions no. 1 and no. 2. It is not presented for the items in question no. 2 because the relationship between conceptual utilization and the organizational structure variables was not significant when multiple linear regression was used, and the relationships between the individual items of question no. 2 and the organizational structure variables were also of significance. Table 7.10 shows a summary of the results of these regression analyses for the items in question no. 1 and the organizational structure variables.

Administrative consultation revealed the highest R^2 in these regression analyses. A further look at these regression analyses reveals that formalization explained 37% of the total explained variance for administrative consultation. In addition, formalization explained 19% of the total explained variance for students' rights, and it explained 22% of the total explained variance for resource development/community change. Formalization is obviously the most important variable in predicting responses to the items in question no. 1 (students' rights, group work, general consultation, resource development/community change, and administrative consultation).

Supplemental Questions

Also of interest are the supplemental questions included on the social workers' questionnaire (Instrument no. 3). These include questions no. 3, no. 7, no. 9, no. 10, no. 12, and no. 14, which are listed in full in the Appendix A.

When social workers were asked in question no. 3 to rate how often they personally performed the activities listed in question no. 1 (instrumental utilization) and question no. 2 (conceptual utilization), the mean of the five Costin activities (personal utilization) was 2.205 with a standard deviation of 0.804, using 137 cases. The mean for personal utilization was less than the mean for

Table 7.11
Prior Knowledge by State

	NUMBER OF DISTRICTS IN SAMPLE	NUMBER WITH PRIOR KNOWLEDGE	PERCENT WITH PRIOR KNOWLEDGE
New York	98	17	.17
North Carolina	63	6	.09
Connecticut	39	22	.56

instrumental utilization (2.392) which is shown in Table 6.5, Chapter 6, and represents utilization by the district as a whole. The mean for personal utilization did correlate positively with both instrumental utilization ($r = 0.84$) and with conceptual utilization ($r = 0.48$). When multiple linear regression analysis was employed between the organizational structure variables and personal utilization, 19% of the variance could be explained. Of these organizational structure variables, formalization explained 15% of the 19% variance in personal utilization. The results suggest that personal utilization is similar to district utilization (questions no. 1 and no. 2), but in all cases it is somewhat less than the district's utilization as a whole.

Of the 112 districts that responded to question no. 7, only forty-five, or 37%, of the districts had a social worker who reported prior knowledge of Costin's recommendation. It is interesting that twenty-two of the forty-five districts, or 49% of the districts, reporting prior knowledge were from the state of Connecticut when Connecticut had the smallest number of districts in the sample. A breakdown of prior knowledge by state is shown in Table 7.11. These results suggest that perhaps there was more dissemination of Costin's study in the state of Connecticut.

Districts which reported prior knowledge of Costin's recommendation did not appear to have a much greater likelihood of reporting instrumental utilization of the recommendation. The correlation was positive but weak, $r = 0.20$. Of the forty-five districts that reported knowledge of Costin's recommendation, thirteen, or 29%, had mean scores for instrumental utilization above 3.0 (a fair amount of use on a scale of 1 to 5). Of the seventy-nine districts that reported no knowledge of Costin's recommendation, twenty-two, or 27%, also had mean instrumental scores above 3.0. The implication here is that prior knowledge is not a significant factor in the utilization of Costin's recommendation. An explanation as to why districts that had not heard of Costin's recommendation

Table 7.12
Perceived Utilization of Costin's Recommendation by Districts Reporting Prior Knowledge

	PERCENT*	NUMBER**
Perceived District Instrumental Utilization	23.3	10
Perceived District Conceptual Utilization	37.21	6
Perceived Personal Instrumental Utilization	48.9	21
Perceived Personal Conceptual Utilization	67.5	29

Percent of respondents reporting a rating of (3) a fair amount, (4) a good deal, or (5) a great deal.
**Total number of respondents is 45.*

utilized it may be that the recommendation was disseminated in a more general fashion without Costin's name attached to it in recent years.

The 45 districts that indicated they had heard of Costin's recommendation prior to the questionnaire were also asked to report its perceived influence on them and their school district in question no. 9 on Instrument no. 3 (see Appendix A). The results are presented in Table 7.12. It is evident that the social workers who reported they had previously heard of Costin's recommendation believed it did have an influence on them. Perceived personal utilization was reported higher than district utilization, which may suggest that it was easier to use Costin's recommendation on an individual basis than to get the district to change or that there is a closer link between knowledge and personal action than between knowledge and district action.

On the supplementary questions (questions no. 10, no. 12, and no. 14 on Instrument no. 3) about the influence of other factors on the pattern of school social work activities performed in their district, one factor was reported by a large percentage of the respondents as having an influence. The passage of Public Law 94-142 was reported by 77.8% of the respondents as having an influence on the pattern of school social work activities in their district. Only 34.1% of the districts reported that the federal budget cuts since 1980 influenced the pattern of school social work activities, and only 10.5% of the districts reported court-ordered desegregation influenced the pattern of school social work activities. None of these factors, however, was correlated significantly with instrumental or conceptual utilization of Costin's recommendation.

Traditional Activities

Although the hypotheses only predicted a relationship between organizational structure variables and utilization of Costin's recommended activities, it was

Table 7.13
The Relationship between the Utilization of Traditional Activities and the
Utilization of Costin's Recommended Activities*

	INSTRUMENTAL UTILIZATION	CONCEPTUAL UTILIZATION	ALL ACTIVITIES
Traditional Social	.1762	.3270	.7150
Work Activities	(140)	(135)	(140)
Question #1	P = .037	P = .001	P = .001
Traditional Social	.1658	.2963	.6272
Work Activities	(135)	(135)	(135)
Question #2	P = .072	P = .001	P = .001

*P is significance level and the number in parentheses is the number of cases.

thought it might be interesting to see how organizational structure variables relate to traditional social work activities. Traditional social work activities are defined as direct services to individual students (1c, 2c), direct services to families (1d, 2d), consultation with teachers on individual students (1e, 2e), interpretation of school social work services (1h, 2h), liaison between the family and community agencies (li, 2i) and social case history (1k, 2k). These activities are further described in Chapter 4.

A correlational analysis using a two-tailed test of significance and a significance level of 0.05 or less was done, with cases with missing data deleted. The analysis showed that traditional activities are not correlated at all with the organizational structure variables of complexity, centralization about policy, centralization about work, formalization, and stratification. They are also not related to the control variables of size, resources, or expenditures.

Table 7.13 shows that the only factors correlated with the traditional activities are the utilization of Costin's recommended activities and the utilization of all activities. The traditional activities in question no. 1 show a very low, positive correlation to the utilization of Costin's recommended activities. The traditional activities in question no. 1 show a positive, high correlation to all eleven activities listed in question no. 1. Similar results are obtained with Costin's recommended activities and all eleven activities.

These results suggest that scores for utilization of traditional activities and utilization of Costin's recommended activities tend to increase together, although the correlations are not strong. The scores for utilization of traditional activities and all activities also tend to increase together with a high correlation. This result is expected since six of the eleven activities in the category of all activities are traditional activities. An additional possibility might be a response bias where

Table 7.14
The Relationship of Organizational Structure Variables to the Performance of All Activities*

	CENTRALIZATION ABOUT POLICY	CENTRALIZATION ABOUT WORK	FORMALIZATION
All Social Work Activities Question #1	-.3043 (100) $P=.002$	-.2594 (99) $P=.009$	-.4837 (100) $P=.001$
All Social Work Activities Question #2	-.1150 (99) $P=.257$	-.0804 (98) $P=.431$	-.1983 (97) $P=.049$

P is significance level and the number in parentheses is the number of cases.

a district social work unit is perceived to do everything, and thus all items are rated highly.

Regression was also used to see if the organizational structure variables could predict the utilization of traditional activities, but nothing was significant at the .05 level or less. This was also to be reflected, since no significant correlations were found between the organizational structure variables and the utilization of the traditional activities.

All Activities

Since Costin's five recommended activities are part of the total eleven activities listed in question no. 1 and question no. 2 (Instrument no. 3), it was thought that there might be a relationship between the organizational structure variables and the total eleven activities. Table 7.14 shows the relationships, using a two-tailed test of significance with a significance level of 0.05 or less and deleting cases with missing data.

There were four significant relationships. All activities on question no. 1 correlated significantly with centralization about policy, centralization about work, and with formalization. All activities on question no. 2 correlated significantly with formalization.

Regression analyses were also done to see how much of the eleven activities could be explained by the organizational structure variables. Table 7.15 shows that 28% of the variance for all activities on question no. 1 could be explained by the organizational structure variables. Formalization contributed over 23% of the variance, and centralization about policy over 3.6% of the variance. The results for all activities on question no. 2 are not significant at the .05 level.

Table 7.15
Regression for All Social Work Activities

STEP	VARIABLE ENTERED	R²	R CHANGE	F	P
1	Formalization	.23393	.23393	16.79476	.000
2	Centralization about Policy	.27047	.03654	10.00991	.000
3	Size	.27444	.00397	6.6823	.001
4	Complexity	.27613	.00169	4.95906	.002
5	Expenditures	.27787	.00174	3.93495	.004
6	Resources	.28335	.00547	3.29482	.008
7	Centralization about Work	.28436	.00102	2.78151	.016

When the results of the correlational and regression analyses for all activities are compared to the results for Costin's recommended activities in Table 7.1, Table 7.5, and Table 7.6, in all cases the correlations and R^2's are higher for Costin's recommended activities than for all activities.

Regrouping the Sample

A regrouping of the sample was done to see if there were any significant differences between high-users of Costin's recommendation and low-users of Costin's recommendation. For the purposes of this analysis, high-users are defined as those districts that had a mean score of 4.0 or more on instrumental utilization. Low-users are defined as those districts that had a mean score of 1.5 or less on instrumental utilization. It is recognized that this is not a random sample and generalizability from this secondary analysis is limited because the assumption of randomness is violated.

There were eleven districts out of 102 matched districts in this sample that could be characterized as low-users and twelve districts that could be characterized as high-users. Table 7.16 shows that the means of low-users and high-users were clearly similar for the organizational structure variables of complexity and stratification and different for the organizational structure variables of centralization about policy, centralization about work, and formalization. In order to see if there were any significant differences in the two groups, t-tests were

Table 7.16
Comparisons of Means of Organizational Structure Variables for Low-Users and High-Users of Costin's Recommendation

VARIABLE	MEAN		STANDARD DEVIATION		T VALUE	DEGREES OF FREEDOM	2-TAILED PROBABILITY
Complexity	.1259	(Low)	.035	(Low)	-.50	21	.621
	.1367	(High)	.067	(High)			
Centralization about Policy	.3624	(Low)	.169	(Low)	2.46	21	.023
	.2075	(High)	.132	(High)			
Centralization about Work	.2183	(Low)	.193	(Low)	1.57	21	.130
	.1262	(High)	.060	(High)			
Formalization	3.7273	(Low)	1.104	(Low)	5.07	21	.000
	1.3333	(High)	1.155	(High)			
Stratification	.3510	(Low)	.051	(Low)	-.43	21	.669
	.3622	(High)	.069	(High)			

performed on the means of the two groups in relation to each organizational structure variable.

The groups differed significantly on formalization and centralization about policy. These are the same two organizational structure variables that contributed significantly to the explanation of variance in the instrumental utilization of Costin's recommended activities as shown in Table 7.5. The results suggest further support for the hypotheses that formalization and centralization about policy are related to the utilization of Costin's recommended activities.

8   *Implications of the Study*

The present investigation was designed to look at the relationship between organizational structure factors and utilization of a research recommendation. This quantitative study employed mailed questionnaires to examine the theory that there is a relationship between the organizational structure factors of complexity, centralization, formalization, and stratification and the utilization of Costin's recommendation (1969a) in the field of school social work. The sample used in the study was a purposive sample of public school districts in three states (New York, North Carolina, and Connecticut). Organizational theory was used as the conceptual framework and a sociological frame of reference was employed. The organization was the unit of analysis.

As a result of the analysis of the data, this chapter will present a synopsis of the findings and their implications for social work. It is divided into six sections which will address the following topics: study findings, practice implications, policy implications, theoretical implications, methodological limitations, and future research.

STUDY FINDINGS

The present study has attempted to answer several questions about the utilization of Costin's research recommendation. The major question was if there was a relationship between the organizational structure of public school districts and utilization of Costin's recommendation. Four subquestions concerning the degree of complexity, degree of centralization, degree of formalization, and degree of stratification, and Costin's research recommendation were also addressed. A fifth subquestion about the influence of the control variables of district size, district resources, and district expenditures was also considered. In addition, secondary analyses of the data provided useful insights and included a current description of the status of school social work and its service delivery methods.

Major Question

In regard to the major question of a relationship between organizational structure and utilization of Costin's recommendation, the multiple linear regression analysis showed that 38% of the variance in instrumental utilization of Costin's recommendation could be explained by organizational structure variables. The two variables with the most importance were formalization, which explained 32.8% of the variance, and centralization about policy, which accounted for 4.1% of the variance. Negligible amounts were contributed by stratification and centralization about work, and complexity was not even in the equation.

In relation to the subquestions, the Pearson product-moment correlations of the hypothesized relationships show significant relationships in four instances. Instrumental utilization was correlated with centralization about policy, with centralization about work, and with formalization. Conceptual utilization was correlated with formalization.

In each of these relationships the direction of the hypothesized relationship was supported by the study. The degree of reported centralization in controlling policy for school social workers was negatively related to instrumental utilization, and the degree of reported centralization defining the activities of school social workers was negatively related to instrumental utilization. The degree of formalization, that is, the degree to which the district had formal rules and regulations controlling school social work activities, was also negatively related to both instrumental and conceptual utilization.

The implication is that two key organizational structural elements, formalization and centralization, have a negative relationship with research utilization. The hypothesis that more decision-making power for the superintendent would result in less research utilization was supported, and the hypothesis that more rules would result in less research utilization was also supported.

The research, however, did not support the hypothesized relationships between degree of complexity and research utilization and between degree of stratification and research utilization. These relationships were not significant for either instrumental or conceptual utilization.

The use of control variables did not have a very important effect on the relationship of the organizational structure variables to research utilization. District size had the most effect, but it was a very small effect. In addition, very little change took place when district size, district resources, or district expenditures were simultaneously controlled.

It is also of interest that different results were obtained for instrumental utilization and conceptual utilization. This means that the Costin activities were more likely to occur as part of actual activities than to be included in job descriptions. It is important to differentiate between different kinds of utilization such as these, and future studies should keep this in mind. The supplementary questions also showed a difference between personal utilization and district utilization (both instrumental and conceptual); personal utilization was reported lower than use in the district as a whole.

Explanations for the lack of significance between degree of complexity and research utilization and between degree of stratification and research utilization can be offered. Most likely the changes need to be made in the way the variables are measured.

In the case of complexity, the definition is number of specialties, but this may not be adequately measured in the present study. When a ratio of specialized personnel (nonclassroom teacher professionals) to all professionals in the district is used, the result may not represent how many different specialties there are. The measure only shows the proportion of specialized positions to total positions in the district; all of the specialized positions may be in one particular specialty. A revision in measurement needs to be considered.

In the case of stratification, revision in measurement may also need to be considered because of possible intervening factors. Stratification is the only independent variable that correlates significantly with all of the control variables. There may be too many other influences on teachers' salaries and superintendents' salaries to make them a good measure of stratification. Not only are the control variables of district size, district resources, and district expenditures involved, but also many school districts follow state salary schedules. Future studies need to look at alternate ways of measuring stratification.

Secondary Analyses

The secondary analyses of the data also contain some interesting findings. The results of each of these will be discussed briefly.

It was found that superintendents' responses and supervisors' responses correlated moderately with each other, but superintendents' responses and social workers' responses did not correlate as highly about centralization about policy and about centralization about work. These different perceptions about organizational structure may need to be examined further in future studies.

When item analyses were done of the individual items in question no. 1 and question no. 2 on the social worker's questionnaire (Instrument no. 3, Appendix A), it was found that all of the items which comprised the variable instrumental utilization correlated highly with instrumental utilization. The items which comprised the variable conceptual utilization had only moderate correlations with conceptual utilization.

When the individual items of question no. 1 and question no. 2 were correlated with the organizational structure variables, formalization and centralization about policy correlated significantly with each of the items in question no. 1. For question no. 2 formalization correlated significantly only with resource development/community change, and centralization about policy correlated significantly only with resource development/community change. The results from the item analysis suggest that there is a stronger relationship between the individual items in question no. 1 (dealing with actual use) and the organizational structure variables than between the individual items in question no. 2 (dealing with job description) and the organizational structure variables.

When an item regression analysis was done between the organizational structure variables and the individual items in question no. 1, administrative consultation revealed the highest R^2, with formalization explaining the largest part of the variance. The results suggest that performing administrative consultation is the strongest individual item correlated with instrumental utilization of Costin's recommendation.

The supplemental questions also showed some interesting patterns. Personal utilization of Costin's recommendation correlated very highly with instrumental utilization and moderately with conceptual utilization. This result suggests that social workers were allowed to perform Costin's recommended activities even if the activities were not listed in official job descriptions (conceptual utilization). It also did not matter whether the respondents to this questionnaire reported that the district had heard specifically of Costin's recommendation or not. There seemed to be an almost equal number of utilizers and nonutilizers of Costin's recommendation who reported prior knowledge of her recommendation. The important implication here is that there is more of a pattern of general dissemination than response to a single report.

Of those that had previously heard of Costin's recommendation, over 67% believed it had an effect on their perceived personal utilization, but only 37% believed it affected their district's perceived utilization. This finding about perceived utilization is in contrast to the earlier high correlation between personal utilization and district utilization.

On the supplementary questions about the influence of other factors on the pattern of school social work activities, the passage of Public Law 94-142, the Education of All Handicapped Children Act of 1975, seemed most important. Three-fourths of all districts reported the law as having an effect on their school social work activities. Although the influence of P.L. 94-142 did not correlate significantly with utilization of Costin's recommendation, its effect needs to be investigated further since it was mentioned by so many districts in the sample.

When the six traditional activities were examined in relation to organizational structure variables, no significant relationships were found. However, when all eleven activities were examined in relation to organizational structure, significant relationships were found for centralization about policy, centralization about work, and formalization. In addition, when regression was utilized, the organizational structure variables explained 28% of the variance for utilization of all activities.

When the sample was divided into two groups of low-users and high-users, the groups differed significantly on two organizational structure variables: formalization and centralization about policy. Although the generalizability of this analysis is limited, it was found that the same two organizational structure variables appeared in this secondary analysis of the important differences in two groups. Thus the analysis provided an additional confirmation of the study's major findings.

Current Status of School Social Work

In addition to the specific findings of the data analysis related to the research questions, this study has presented an updated look at the current status of school social work and its service delivery pattern. The present view is very different than what Costin found in 1969.

Costin's (1969a) study reported that school social workers were not responding to the concerns of the time and were ignoring the pressing problems of the school population, the social conditions underlying the problems, and the relationship of the school to other social institutions. The activity of casework service was assigned the most importance by respondents in her study and the factor leadership and policy-making was assigned the least importance.

In the present study, the traditional activities of school social work were defined as direct services to individual students, direct services to families, consultation with teachers on individual students, interpretation of school social work services, liaison between the family and community agencies, and the social case history. These traditional activities are still performed in nearly all school social work settings, as shown in Table 6.5, Chapter 6, and they are still part of school social work job descriptions, as shown in Table 6.6. What is different is that Costin's recommended activities are also being performed and included in job descriptions. Costin's recommended activities include students' rights, group work, consultation to teachers on general issues, resource development/community change, and consultation with administrators in formulation of administrative policy.

Table 6.5 provides a closer look at the individual items in Costin's recommended activities, and it shows that for this sample the most frequently performed activity from Costin's recommendation is group work. Group work is followed by general consultation, administrative consultation, resource development/community change, and students' rights. No longer is administrative consultation or the idea of policy-making the factor of least importance, as the Costin (1969a) study reported; administrative consultation, in fact, was the strongest of the Costin activities among high-users.

When one looks at the districts that had high utilization scores (mean utilization score of 4.0 or more), only twelve districts fall into this category. The score of 4.0 was chosen because it represents the response of "a good deal" of use. Similarly, only eleven districts which had mean utilization scores of 1.5 or less. The score of 1.5 represents the response of "very little" use. The other seventy-nine districts in this matched sample of 102 districts fall somewhere in between the high-users and the low-users. These results suggest that there are a great many districts in a middle range of utilization of Costin's recommendation and not very many at either end of extreme use or nonuse.

When the high-users are examined more, it is clear that they are performing not only Costin's recommended activities, but they are also performing the traditional activities as well. The means of the traditional activities are very similar for the low-users, high-users, and all-users. Thus, it was expected that no significant difference was found between low-users and high-users on traditional activities. The high-users perform both traditional activities and Costin's recommended activities.

What the current study has done is present a picture of the pattern of school social work activities in the sample. First, traditional school social work activities are still being performed, and they are performed frequently. Secondly, Costin's recommended activities are also being performed. Costin's recommended activities are performed in addition to (not to the exclusion of) traditional activities. There are a few high-user districts and a few low-user districts; however, most districts fall in the mid-range of utilization of Costin's recommended activities with group work—that is, work with groups of students around common problems, being the Costin activity most widely added.

The current study reveals a mixed approach to social service delivery in the schools. School social work practice presently includes both traditional activities and Costin's recommended activities. For further discussion of these service delivery issues see Chavkin (1985, 1989, 1991).

Summary

In summary this study tried to answer the major question of whether or not a relationship existed between organizational structure variables and the utilization of Costin's recommendation. The study employed organizational theory as its conceptual basis; it used a broad definition of utilization; it utilized a quantitative methodology in one content area; and it focused on specific organizational structure variables.

The results of both the major and secondary analyses of the data suggest that for the present sample formalization and centralization about policy are important factors in whether school districts utilized Costin's research recommendation. A higher level of formalization, or rules which govern social work practice, is associated with a lower level of research utilization, and a lower level of formalization is associated with a higher level of research utilization. A higher level of centralization, or the decision-making power of the superintendent in the area of social work policies, is associated with a lower level of research utilization, and a lower level of centralization is associated with a higher level of research utilization. The results also provide an overview of the current pattern of school social work activities and suggest a mixed model of both traditional and Costin's recommended activities.

PRACTICE IMPLICATIONS

The major practical relevance of the study is that it helps school social workers understand more about organizational structure factors that facilitate and inhibit utilization of research recommendations. It is essential that school social workers are aware of the organizations in which they work.

Social workers in more formalized and centralized districts are more likely to be limited to traditional activities and less likely to undertake activities originally recommended by Costin. Social workers in such districts would therefore likely have to develop a more elaborate strategy for introducing change than social workers in districts in which there were less rules and less central control.

Based on this research about the organizational perspective on social work practice, there are clear implications not only for social workers in schools but to all social workers. As discussed in Chavkin (1986), the following recommendations relate to all social workers regardless of the type of organization in which they work.

1. Social workers should find out how power is distributed in their organization. They need to know who has the most and least influence in decision making.

2. Social workers should examine the extent to which rules govern their daily work. They need to know who makes the rules and how rules are changed in their organization.

3. Social workers should be aware of the diversity of knowledge and expertise in their organizations. They need to look at the advantages and disadvantages of the number of occupational specialties in organizations.

4. Social workers should consider how rewards are distributed to their organizations. They need to know how advancement and merit are achieved.

5. Social workers need to look for possible links between organizational structure factors, particularly formalization and centralization, and their utilization of research.

Social work is an organizationally based profession where social workers are influenced by the organizations in which they work. This case example of school social work and the utilization of Costin's recommendation (1969a) has shown that there is an important organizational connection related to the structure of the organization where social workers are employed. Organizational structure has a potent influence on social workers, and social workers need to pay attention to organizational context of their work.

In addition, school administrators (whether sympathetic or hostile to external research utilization) may find the results of this study useful when they are making organizational changes. They need to be cognizant of the possible negative effect that more rules and more centralization will have on their district's utilization of research and development of innovation in a specialty service unit like school social work.

Researchers may also find the results of this study useful both in designing future research projects and in making policy recommendations that take into account organizational structure. Researchers can benefit by initially placing research projects in organizations that are less formalized and less centralized. The study may also aid those in the research-dissemination process in distinguishing organizations that are more receptive (or less receptive) to research utilization. For example, in selecting school districts for pilot studies or experimental programs, it would be helpful to know that rule-oriented and centralized school districts have less chance of utilizing research and that less formalized and less centralized districts have a better chance of utilizing research.

Social work educators who are either preparing students for school social work or working with the continuing education of practicing school social workers may also find the current study relevant. Social work students and practitioners need to be aware of research utilization and how organizational structures can influence it. In addition, the research curricula for all social work students could be enriched with empirical evidence of organizational utilization and nonutilization of research.

The updated view of the status of school social work service delivery is also important to both the curricula for future school social workers and to the present field of practitioners. School social workers are performing Costin's recommended activities, and these skill areas need to be further addressed in both schools of social work and continuing education programs. This study is well-supported by the work of leading scholars Allen-Meares, Washington, and Welsh (1986), Freeman and Pennekamp (1988), and Winters and Easton (1983). Generalist approaches and casework methods are not sufficient to meet the challenges of leadership for performing in the areas of consultation to administrators, resource development/community change, students' rights, group work, and general consultation with teachers. For discussion of current social work practice roles, see Allen-Meares, Washington, and Welsh (1986), Levine, Allen-Meares, and Easton (1987), Chavkin and Brown (1992), Chavkin and Garza-Lubeck (1988), Nystrom (1988), Franklin and Streeter (1991), Kennedy and Chavkin (1992).

In summary, the current study has many implications for practice. Most significant, it has contributed to an awareness of the important relationship between organizational structure and social workers' utilization of Costin's research recommendation. It will help social workers understand more about the influence of the organizations in which they work.

POLICY IMPLICATIONS

In light of the rise in cost and number of research projects, the present study has important policy implications because it examines factors that may affect the utilization of research. It is critical that government agencies and taxpayers know more about these factors that influence the use of research in order to decide how much and what kinds of research to support. It is a waste of taxpayers' money and agency time to fund research projects and dissemination efforts in organizations that are not conducive to research utilization. The present study suggests that research projects in school districts have a better chance for utilization when the districts are less formalized and less centralized. Thus, policies should be directed toward funding and disseminating research initially in school districts with less formalization and less centralization.

The organizational structure variables of formalization and centralization were even more important than whether districts had heard specifically of Costin's recommendation or not. Just knowing about a research recommendation does not increase the likelihood of its use. Low formalization and low centralization were better predictors of utilization.

The present study also enhances the understanding of the research-policy linkage discussed by Zurcher and Bonjean (1970). Because Costin's research recommendation makes a policy recommendation about a change in a social service delivery approach, this study suggests that policy changes can be influenced by research recommendations and these recommendations for change have a better chance of being utilized in less formalized and less centralized school districts. This finding shows that the relationship between research and policy may not always be as uncertain as Rein (1976), Weiss (1977), Lynn (1978), and others have posed. Formalization and centralization are two factors that affected the linkage between research and policy in this study.

THEORETICAL IMPLICATIONS

The most important theoretical implication of the current study lies in its specific contribution to the conceptualization of research utilization for social workers. The works of Tripodi, Fellin, and Meyer (1969), Zimbalist (1977), Mullen (1978), and Rothman (1980) present individual and extraorganizational perspectives on research utilization, but little consideration has previously been given to an organizational perspective.

The current study suggests a negative relationship between formalization and research utilization and between centralization about policy and research utilization. These organizational structure characteristics had an impact on whether or not school social workers in a district reported utilization of Costin's recommendation. The conceptualization of research utilization must include an organizational perspective.

The subject of organizational structure and utilization of a research recommendation also encompasses a myriad of other theories about organizations, innovations, and sociology of knowledge. Each of these theoretical implications is important and will be discussed.

The current study has extended organizational theory by relating Hage and Aiken's (1970) structural variables to research utilization. While Hage and Aiken established relationships between centralization, complexity, formalization, and stratification and program change, this study has linked the structural variables of formalization and centralization to a more specific organizational behavior— the utilization of a research recommendation. The results of this study are in accord with the ideas of Abbott (1965), V. Thompson (1965), and Bennis (1971) who suggest that the modern bureaucratic structures of organizations such as schools inhibit the utilization of new ideas. Rule-oriented and centralized school districts were found to be the least likely to use Costin's research recommendation. The current study has supported the previous idea that organizational structure can be a major impediment to the flow of knowledge by specifically focusing on the relationship of organizational structure variables and the utilization of a research recommendation.

The present study has also enhanced work on innovation and knowledge utilization. Havelock's earlier report (1971) on innovation, dissemination, and knowledge focused on the two competing themes of maintaining order and innovating; both concern structure from opposite perspectives. Havelock suggested that maintaining order led to increased structural barriers for knowledge flow and innovating demanded decreased structural barriers for knowledge flow. The present study has shown that formalization and centralization are associated with low utilization of Costin's research recommendation.

In accord with this study's focus on the application of social science research, it has also contributed to what Merton (1949) called the need for a thorough study of applied social science. Others such as Lazarsfjeld and his colleagues (1967) have worked on a ''theory of uses'' and Holzner (1978) and Holzner and Marx (1979) have called for a systematic study of a sociology of knowledge application. The present examination of the relationship between organizational structure variables and utilization of Costin's research recommendation has associated formalization and centralization about policy with the use of Costin's recommendation. The study suggests the need to include organizational structure variables in theories about uses and knowledge application.

In addition, to the theoretical implications in the areas of organizational structure and research utilization, the updated view of current school social work practice also has some theoretical implications in terms of a definition of the field. Costin (1969a) labeled the definition of school social work as ''static'' and ''reflecting a residual conceptualization of social welfare.'' Meares (1977) saw school social work with a ''transitional'' definition of practice.

The current study, however, presents a ''mixed'' definition, which is different from either Costin's or Meares's views. The current study found that school social workers are using both traditional activities and Costin's recommended activities. The field is very active in all activities; even districts that are high-users of Costin's recommended activities perform traditional activities frequently. The term ''static'' does not apply now. In addition, the word ''transitional'' seems inappropriate since it implies that eventually school social work might be moving toward using Costin's recommended activities exclusively, and there is no evidence in this study to support this as a possible future stage.

The "mixed" definition supports an earlier 1980 study by Lambert and Mullaly (1982) in Toronto, Ontario. They found that school social workers do not place importance on one focus (individual change or systems change) but recognize both. The "mixed" definition of school social work service delivery adds to the understanding of the current field of school social work.

In summary, the current study has many theoretical implications. Because this study has shown an association between organizational structure variables and the utilization of a research recommendation, it needs to be replicated and extended in order to continue to add to theory.

METHODOLOGICAL LIMITATIONS

There are several limitations to this study that need to be considered, and caution needs to be observed in generalizing the results. Some of the limitations arise directly from the researcher's assumptions that the responses represent reality, and these assumptions should be noted. Other limitations which must be acknowledged occur because of time and cost restraints.

First, the data are all from self-report, and the reporters may be biased. The data are also all from written, mailed responses. It is possible that people respond differently when they have to write a response down and mail it. In addition, the instruments are brief. Perhaps longer instruments would have allowed more opportunity for cross-checking of responses. Attempts were made to lessen the effect of all of these limitations by conducting a pretest and by checking documentable sources with perceived responses whenever possible.

Due to financial constraints, the number of states from which the sample was selected and the sample size itself was necessarily limited. Future studies might be able to improve the generalizability of the study by including more states or perhaps a different kind of state. Replication of the study definitely needs to be done to include other areas of the country and other types of organizations to test the reliability of the findings.

Also there has been disagreement about the use of multiple linear regression with ordinal level data because rank-ordered data violate the assumptions of multiple linear regression. However, as Labovitz (1970, 1972) suggests, there is more to be gained than lost in the judicious application of multiple linear regression to ordinal level data.

FUTURE RESEARCH

As a result of this investigation a number of suggestions for future research are evident. One set of suggestions pertains to replication and revision of the present study, and another set of suggestions, perhaps the most important, focuses on the more general issues surrounding organizational influences on patterns of social service delivery.

Replications could include a wider range of school districts and states, or perhaps a different kind of sample, in order to increase the generalized ability of the results. Longitudinal studies would also be useful in order to see the effects of time on utilization, and additional variables could also be considered.

In the current study, the different results for instrumental and conceptual utilization point to the continuing need to define utilization more specifically. The use of more measures for determining utilization would also be helpful in extending knowledge about levels and kinds of utilization.

Since little change was noted when the controls of size, resources, and expenditures were used, additional controls may need to be considered in future studies. These controls might include features of the work setting or individual characteristics of the superintendent, supervisor, or the school social work unit.

Because this study has employed a quantitative approach, future studies should also include qualitative approaches. It would be helpful to interview social workers and superintendents concerning both their perception about utilization of Costin's recommendation and their perception about organizational structure.

Future studies might also look further at all the organizational characteristics of districts where high utilization of Costin's research recommendation is reported. It would be useful to know if high utilization districts are similar in other organizational characteristics.

As far as measurement of variables, some more study is needed. The measurement of complexity and stratification, as discussed earlier, needs revision. It would be helpful with the other variables to explore other ways of measuring them and see if the same results are obtained.

In addition, the influence of P.L. 94-142 both on organizational structure and on utilization of Costin's research recommendation needs to be examined further. This law was reported to have an effect on the pattern of school social work activities in many districts. Both the nature and the extent of this effect needs to be analyzed because it may well contribute to the relationship between organizational structure and utilization of Costin's research recommendation.

In addition to replicating and revising the present study, future research should examine the more general issues surrounding organizational influences on patterns of school social service delivery. The focus of future research needs to be broadened to include organizational influences on other current school social service delivery patterns. Some of the delivery patterns that need to be examined further in relation to organizational factors are these: the use of interdisciplinary teams, the use of volunteers, the use of bachelor level social workers (B.S.W.'s), and the use of contractual social workers from outside the school district. Each of these needs to be examined in relation to organizational structure and/or other organizational factors.

Future research should also look at additional forms of service-provision innovations and their relationship to organizational factors. These innovations might be in the area of service delivery methods, but they could also be in several other areas. For instance, the size of individual worker's caseloads in a district might be affected by how the school was structured. Specific treatment approaches (behaviorist vs. psychosocial) of a social work unit might be influenced by other organizational factors. The list of possibilities includes how evaluations are conducted, the size of the social work unit, the population served, and many other varied aspects of school social work.

The important point is that the thrust of future research needs to be toward understanding more about the very complex relationship of research and social work practice. The organizational perspective has been shown to be an important one in the case of Costin's recommendation and the social work field needs to look at the organizational perspective in relation to other research recommendations.

APPENDICES

Questionnaires

INSTRUMENT NO. 1

SUPERINTENDENT'S QUESTIONNAIRE *

PLEASE ANSWER THE QUESTIONS CAREFULLY.

1. How much influence or say does each of the following have on a decision about the content of the <u>job description</u> of the school social worker in your district?

Very Little = 1   Some = 2   A Fair Amount = 3   A Good Deal =4   A Great Deal = 5

a. superintendent	1 2 3 4 5
b. central office administrative staff	1 2 3 4 5
c. social work supervisor or immediate supervisor	1 2 3 4 5
d. social worker	1 2 3 4 5

2. How much influence or say does each of the following have on a decision about how the actual pattern of <u>daily activities</u> is carried out by the school social worker in your district?

Very Little = 1   Some = 2   A Fair Amount = 3   A Good Deal =4   A Great Deal = 5

a. superintendent	1 2 3 4 5
b. central office administrative staff	1 2 3 4 5
c. social work supervisor or immediate supervisor	1 2 3 4 5
d. social worker	1 2 3 4 5

3. How much is the daily practice of a school social worker determined by formal written rules and definitions of procedures in your district?

Very Little = 1   Some = 2   A Fair Amount = 3   A Good Deal =4   A Great Deal = 5

a. superintendent	1	2	3	4	5
b. central office administrative staff	1	2	3	4	5
c. social work supervisor or immediate supervisor	1	2	3	4	5
d. social worker	1	2	3	4	5

4. What is the total number of certified professionals (employees with a B.A. or higher) currently employed by your district?

5. How many of the above certified professionals have job titles other than classroom teacher?

6. What is the annual salary (12 mo.) of the superintendent in your district?

7. What is the salary of an entry-level B.A. teacher in your district? Please state 9, 10, 11, 12 month or other basis of employment.

8. What was your district's student enrollment in September?

9. What is your current job title?

THANK YOU FOR YOUR VALUABLE TIME. PLEASE PLACE A CHECK MARK TO THE RIGHT OF THIS QUESTION IF YOU WOULD LIKE A COPY OF THE RESULTS.

*This is an approximate reproduction of the original questionnaire. An earlier version of the questionnaire contained boxes to check responses instead of numbers to circle.

INSTRUMENT NO. 2

SUPERVISOR'S QUESTIONNAIRE*

PLEASE ANSWER THE QUESTIONS CAREFULLY.

1. How much influence or say does each of the following have on a decision about the content of the job description of the school social worker in your district?

Very Little = 1 Some = 2 A Fair Amount = 3 A Good Deal =4   A Great Deal = 5

a. superintendent   1 2 3 4 5
b. central office administrative staff   1 2 3 4 5
c. social work supervisor or immediate supervisor   1 2 3 4 5
d. social worker   1 2 3 4 5

2. How much influence or say does each of the following have on a decision about how the actual pattern of <u>daily activities</u> is carried out by the school social worker in your district?

Very Little = 1 Some = 2 A Fair Amount = 3 A Good Deal =4   A Great Deal = 5

a. superintendent   1 2 3 4 5
b. central office administrative staff   1 2 3 4 5
c. social work supervisor or immediate supervisor   1 2 3 4 5
d. social worker   1 2 3 4 5

3. How much is the daily practice of a school social worker determined by formal written rules and definitions of procedures in your district?

Very Little = 1 Some = 2 A Fair Amount = 3 A Good Deal =4   A Great Deal = 5

a. superintendent   1 2 3 4 5
b. central office administrative staff   1 2 3 4 5
c. social work supervisor or immediate supervisor   1 2 3 4 5
d. social worker   1 2 3 4 5

4. What is the total number of certified professionals (employees with a B.A. or higher) currently employed by your district?

5. How many of the above certified professionals have job titles other than classroom teacher?

6. What is the annual salary (12 mo.) of the superintendent in your district?

7. What is the salary of an entry-level B.A. teacher in your district? Please state 9, 10, 11, 12 month or other basis of employment.

8. What was your district's student enrollment in September?

9. What is your current job title?

THANK YOU FOR YOUR VALUABLE TIME. PLEASE PLACE A CHECK MARK TO THE RIGHT OF THIS QUESTION IF YOU WOULD LIKE A COPY OF THE RESULTS.

*This is an approximate reproduction of the original questionnaire. An earlier version of the questionnaire contained boxes to check responses instead of numbers to circle.

INSTRUMENT NO. 3
SCHOOL SOCIAL WORKER'S QUESTIONNAIRE*

PLEASE READ THE FOLLOWING QUESTIONS CAREFULLY. YOUR RESPONSES WILL HELP US UNDERSTAND MORE ABOUT THE CURRENT STATE OF SCHOOL SOCIAL WORK.

1. How often are the following <u>activities performed</u> as part of the total school social work function in your school district over the normal academic year?

Very Little = 1 Some = 2 A Fair Amount = 3 A Good Deal =4   A Great Deal = 5

a. work with parents on students' rights issues	1 2 3 4 5
b. group work with students	1 2 3 4 5
c. direct services to individual students	1 2 3 4 5
d. direct services to families	1 2 3 4 5
e. consultation with teachers on individual students	1 2 3 4 5
f. consultation with teachers on general classroom issues	1 2 3 4 5
g. assistance with resource development and planned change in the community	1 2 3 4 5
h. interpretation of school social work services	1 2 3 4 5
i. liaison between the family and community agencies	1 2 3 4 5
j. consultation with school administrators in formulation of administrative policy	1 2 3 4 5
k. social case history	1 2 3 4 5

2. Are the following <u>activities specifically identified</u> in the operational description of school social work in your district?

1 = No, 2 = Yes, 3 = Not Sure

a. work with parents on students' rights issues	1 2 3
b. group work with students	1 2 3
c. direct services to individual students	1 2 3
d. direct services to families	1 2 3
e. consultation with teachers on individual students	1 2 3
f. consultation with teachers on general classroom issues	1 2 3
g. assistance with resource development and planned change in the community	1 2 3
h. interpretation of school social work services	1 2 3
i. liaison between the family and community agencies	1 2 3
j. consultation with school administrators in formulation of administrative policy	1 2 3
k. social case history	1 2 3

3. How often do you personally perform the following activities as part of your school social work function over the normal academic year?

Very Little = 1 Some = 2 A Fair Amount = 3 A Good Deal = 4 A Great Deal = 5

a. work with parents on students' rights issues	1 2 3 4 5
b. group work with students	1 2 3 4 5
c. direct services to individual students	1 2 3 4 5
d. direct services to families	1 2 3 4 5
e. consultation with teachers on individual students	1 2 3 4 5
f. consultation with teachers on general classroom issues	1 2 3 4 5
g. assistance with resource development and planned change in the community	1 2 3 4 5
h. interpretation of school social work services	1 2 3 4 5
i. liaison between the family and community agencies	1 2 3 4 5
j. consultation with school administrators in formulation of administrative policy	1 2 3 4 5
k. social case history	1 2 3 4 5

4. How much influence or say does each of the following have on a decision about the content of the job description of the school social worker in your district?

Very Little = 1 Some = 2 A Fair Amount = 3 A Good Deal =4 A Great Deal = 5

a. superintendent	1 2 3 4 5
b. central office administrative staff	1 2 3 4 5
c. social work supervisor or immediate supervisor	1 2 3 4 5
d. social worker	1 2 3 4 5

5. How much influence or say does each of the following have on a decision about how the actual pattern of daily activities is carried out by the school social worker in your district?

Very Little = 1 Some = 2 A Fair Amount = 3 A Good Deal =4 A Great Deal = 5

a. superintendent   1 2 3 4 5
b. central office administrative staff   1 2 3 4 5
c. social work supervisor or immediate supervisor   1 2 3 4 5
d. social worker   1 2 3 4 5

6. How much is the daily practice of a school social worker determined by formal written rules and definitions of procedures in yur district?

Very Little = 1 Some = 2 A Fair Amount = 3 A Good Deal =4 A Great Deal = 5

7. In 1969 Professor Lela Costin in an article in the Social Service Review reported on a research study of the task activities of school social workers. As a result of that study she recommended that the traditional casework emphasis in school social work was outmoded and a new approach, which looked at the whole school, was needed. Her recommendation was for a social change approach, which focused on the student's environment. The home, school, and community were to be involved in the educational process, and the school social worker was to play a redefined and more active role with administrators.

Have you heard of Professor Costin's recommendation before?

IF ANSWER TO QUESTION NO.7 IS YES PLEASE GO ON TO QUESTIONS NO.8 AND 9. IF ANSWER IS NO OR NOT SURE, SKIP TO QUESTION NO.10.

8. Please explain how and approximately when you heard about Professor Costin's recommendation.

9. How much has the recommendation in Professor Costin's article influenced

Very Little = 1 Some = 2 A Fair Amount = 3 A Good Deal =4 A Great Deal = 5

a. specific programs and activities of your district's social work unit?
b. thinking and ideas about school social work practice in your district's social work unit?
c. the pattern of your personal school social work professional practice?
d. your personal thinking and ideas about school social work?

.10. Has the passage of P.L. 94-142 influenced the pattern of school social work activities performed in your district?

11. If the answer to question No.10 is yes, please explain or comment below.

12. Have the federal budget cuts since 1980 influenced the pattern of school social work activities performed in your district?

13. If the answer to question No.12 is yes, please explain or comment below.

14. Has court-ordered desegregation influenced the pattern of school social work activities performed in your district?

15. If the answer to question No.14 is yes, please explain or comment below.

16. How long have school social work services been available in your school district?

If less than fifteen years, please comment on the reasons why they were initiated.

17. What is the total number of certified professionals (employees with a B.A. or higher) currently employed by your district?

18. How many of the above certified professional have job titles other than classroom teachers?

19. What is the annual salary (12 mo.) of the superintendent in your district?

20. What is the salary of an entry-level, B.A. teacher in your district? Please state 9, 10, 11, 12 month or other basis of employment.

21. Please list your

educational degree(s)

institution(s)

date(s) of degree(s)

22. Please list your current job title:

THANK YOU FOR YOUR VALUABLE TIME. PLEASE PUT A CHECK MARK TO THE RIGHT IF YOU WOULD LIKE TO RECEIVE A COPY OF THE RESULTS.

*This is an approximate reproduction of the original questionnaire. An earlier version of the questionnaire contained boxes to check responses instead of numbers to circle.

PROCEDURE FOR RANKING RESOURCES

New York
Mean Resources Per Pupil $1,602
75% of Mean Resources $1,200
125% of Mean Resources $2,000

Districts with   0–$1,199 Mean Resources assigned 1
Districts with $1,200–$1,601 Mean Resources assigned 2
Districts with $1,602–$1,999 Mean Resources assigned 3
Districts with $2,000–above   Mean Resources assigned 4

North Carolina
Mean Resources Per Pupil $835
75% of Mean Resources $625
125% of Mean Resources $1,045

Districts with   0–$625 Mean Resources assigned 1
Districts with $626–$834 Mean Resources assigned 2
Districts with $835–$1,044 Mean Resources assigned 3
Districts with $1,045–above   Mean Resources assigned 4

Connecticut
Mean Resources Per Pupil $2,060
75% of Mean Resources $1,645
125% of Mean Resources $2,475

Districts with   0–$1,644 Mean Resources assigned 1
Districts with $1,644–$2,059 Mean Resources assigned 2
Districts with $2,060–$2,474 Mean Resources assigned 3
Districts with $2,475–above   Mean Resources assigned 4

New York
Mean Expenditure Per Pupil $2,381
75% of Mean Expenditure $1,786
125% of Mean Expenditure $2,977

Districts with   0–$1,785 Mean Expenditure assigned 1
Districts with $1,786–$2,380 Mean Expenditure assigned 2
Districts with $2,381–$2,976 Mean Expenditure assigned 3
Districts with $2,977–above   Mean Expenditure assigned 4

North Carolina
Mean Expenditure Per Pupil $1,944
75% of Mean Expenditure $1,458
125% of Mean Expenditure $2,430

Districts with   0–$1,457 Mean Expenditure assigned 1
Districts with $1,458–$1,943 Mean Expenditure assigned 2
Districts with $1,944–$2,429 Mean Expenditure assigned 3
Districts with $2,430–above   Mean Expenditure assigned 4

Connecticut
Mean Expenditure Per Pupil $2,489
75% of Mean Expenditure $1,867
125% of Mean Expenditure $3,110

Districts with   0–$1,866 Mean Expenditure assigned 1
Districts with $1,867–$2,488 Mean Expenditure assigned 2
Districts with $2,489–$3,110 Mean Expenditure assigned 3
Districts with $3,111–above   Mean Expenditure assigned 4

APPENDIX B

An Analysis of the Tasks in School Social Work

Lela B. Costin

University of Illinois, Urbana

ABSTRACT

A definition of school social work practice was developed from opinions expressed by professional school social workers about the relative importance of different parts of their work for the attainment of social work goals within a public school setting. It is a matter of concern that this definition strongly suggests the main body of tasks and goals in school social work is not attuned to the urgent problems of school children and youth today. Nor does it appear to provide a promising basis for experimentation in assigning responsibilities to social work staff with different levels of education.

This study sought to answer two questions: How do professional social workers define content of school social work and the relative importance of its parts? Does such a definition provide a promising basis for experimentation in assigning responsibilities to social work staff with different levels of education or training? Two current and generally recognized problems provided the stimulus for this study: (a) unsolved questions concerning the recruitment and utilization of social work personnel (4,6) and (b) disturbing conditions in the public schools which have implications for the nature of an effective school social work service (1,3).

METHOD

A comprehensive list was assembled of tasks known to be contained in activities of school social workers or implied by professional goals and principles of education and social work. Each task was written in behavioral terms to describe a specific activity in relation to children, parents, teachers, administrators, or other school personnel, as well as community agencies and interest groups.

Originally published as Lela B. Costin, "An Analysis of the Tasks in School Social Work," *Social Service Review*, 43, 1969, 274–85. Reprinted by permission of the University of Chicago Press. Copyright 1969 by University of Chicago. All rights reserved.

This study was financed in part by Grant No. OEG 3-6-068315-1306 from the United States Department of Health, Education, and Welfare, Office of Education, Bureau of Research, Project No. 6-8315. See (5).

The tasks were translated into a rating of 107 items, each item being a specific task of the school social worker. Respondents answered two basic questions in relation to each task. The first question was, "How important do you consider the task for the attainment of social work goals within a school system?" Respondents indicated their opinion on a four-point scale from 0 (not important) to 3 (very important). The second question asked was, "Can the task appropriately be assigned to a person with less than your level of education or professional preparation?" Respondents indicated their opinions on a four-point scale indicating whether a task could "never," "occasionally," "frequently," or "always" be assigned to a person with less education and professional preparation than their own. The purpose of this second question was to determine which tasks professional school social workers are inclined to surrender willingly to "nonprofessional" staff at some lower level of education and training. Such information could provide obvious and acceptable tasks with which to try out differential assignments.

Since no central registry of social workers employed in school systems was available, lists were assembled for each of the various states by correspondence with state departments of public instruction, faculty members of graduate schools of social work, and known school social workers in supervisory positions. Names were obtained from forty states and the District of Columbia. The lists were complete for twenty-nine states (that is, they contained the names of all social workers employed in public schools) and partially complete for another six states. Five other states were found to employ a very small number of school social workers—three persons or fewer; most of these names were obtained. The remaining ten states did not have any professional school social workers employed.

The roster of school social workers was then checked against the 1966 *NASW Directory* for each person's membership as a means of confirming graduate social work education or its equivalent. This procedure resulted in a list of 1,456 persons with National Association of Social Workers membership employed or active in school social work in forty states and the District of Columbia. A sample of 368 names—approximately 25%— was selected as follows: From the separate state rosters which listed four or more persons, every fourth name from the alphabetical list was drawn; for rosters of states listing three or two social workers, the second name was drawn; if a state's roster showed only one name, that single name was drawn.

Data were collected between December 1, 1966, and March 31, 1967. Fourteen questionnaires were returned for lack of forwarding addresses. Of the remaining 354 potential respondents, 257 (72.5 percent) returned their questionnaires. Nineteen questionnaires were incomplete and therefore excluded. There remained a total of 238 questionnaires for analysis. For studies using mail questionnaires, these data represent a substantial return.

The first data analyzed were answers to the question, "How do you consider the task for the attainment of social work goals within a school system?" A factor analyses was carried out.[1] The method of principal axes analysis was used, the factors and loadings being produced by rotation, using the varimax technique.[2]

Data from the second part of the questionnaire consisted of responses to the question, "Can the task appropriately be assigned to a person with less than your level of education and professional preparation?" Mean ratings for each item were computed, as well as the overall means for each group of items within a factor, and comparisons made of relative "assignability" of the factor groups of tasks.

DESCRIPTION OF FACTORS

Factor analysis revealed a meaningful structure among the school social work tasks. Nine factors emerged. (No task was retained as part of a factor unless it loaded at least .40 on that factor. Twenty-five items loaded less than .40. No factor contained less than five items.) The Appendix [to this reprinted article] contains a list of the tasks in each of the nine factors.

Casework service to the child and his parents. This factor defined a way of offering help to the individual child and his parents in relation to the child's personal problems. The approach is a generally supportive one, and the emphasis is on diagnosis, clarification of the problems with other school personnel and with parents, and work with the child concerning his feelings, attitudes, and relationships to adults and other significant persons in his life.

Caseload management. Tasks included in this factor typify fairly routine tasks necessary to an effective and well-organized day-by-day management of work load.

Interpreting school social work service. The principal aim of tasks which make up this factor is to interpret, clarify, and coordinate school social work services with other special services within a school system.

Clinical treatment of children with emotional problems. This factor contains tasks which represent a treatment relationship to the child. Through use of a casework relationship or the group process, the worker helps the child to gain insight into his emotional problems, to develop his personal goals and values, and to change his behavior in life situations. Work with the child's parents is not represented in this factor.

Liaison between the family and community agencies. Tasks contained in this factor appear to measure the role of the school social worker acting as a liaison between a child and his parents and the existing community agencies. Emphasis is upon obtaining information about an individual family's functioning or experiences of community agencies in relation to that family, with active support offered to the child and his family in the use of community agencies. The focus is upon the individual child and family and their use of existing community resources. This differs from the "community service" items in the factor called "Leadership and policy-making," which reflect responsibility for community planning and social change.

Interpreting the child to the teacher. The school social work tasks which compose this factor are ones that find the social worker acting mainly to help the teacher understand a specific child in relation to the use of school social work service. This factor has not been called "consultation with the teacher," since the tasks seem designed to facilitate use of school social work service in relation to a particular child, rather than consultation for a broader school purpose.

Educational counseling with the child and his parent. School social work tasks included in this factor describe a kind of work with the individual child and his parents which is oriented toward the school's educational function. This factor includes explanation and clarification of the school's social and academic expectations and of its authority, help to parents for improving their relationship to the school, and help to the child in the area of his educational goals, values, abilities, and interests.

Leadership and policy-making. This factor appeared to measure school social work responsibility for professional leadership in relation to the school and community, and service to the school administration in the area of pupil-welfare policy. High loadings were found on those tasks having to do with the status of the social work and education professions, consultation with school administrators, community services in relation to social planning and social action, and work with groups of parents about their school concerns.

Personal service to the teacher. Tasks included in this factor seem related to those described in the factor, "Interpreting the child to the teacher." These appear to measure activity of the school social worker in relation to a teacher's personal problems as they affect her interactions with a child in her classroom, or as they interfere in other ways with her work. This factor is omitted from further discussion of findings because it appears to represent a "rejected" set of tasks, that is, tasks which were rated very low in importance, with frequent marginal comments by respondents suggesting that these tasks were inappropriate for a school social worker's activity.

RELATIVE IMPORTANCE OF SCHOOL
SOCIAL WORK TASKS

On the basis of the response to the question, "How important do you consider the attainment of social work goals within a school system?" a mean rating was computed for each of the 107 items on the scale, as well as the overall mean for each group of items within a factor.[3] Ratings were as follows: 0—not important; 1—slightly important; 2—moderately important; 3—very important. Table B.1 shows the factor means, ranked from high to low, and the significant differences among these means.

As shown in Table B.1, school social workers assigned significantly greater importance to the tasks that make up Factor 2, "Casework service to the child and his parents," than to the tasks in any other factor. By contrast, the tasks of Factor 1, "Leadership and policy-making," were assigned significantly less importance than those in any other factor.

Inspection of items contained in the six most highly rated factors (Factors 2, 5, 6, 7, 8, and 9) indicates that school social workers formulated a definition of their work which was focused primarily upon the individual child in relation to his emotional problem and his personal adjustment. The following findings are of special interest:

1. Service to the child included the use of casework or group work, although casework was rated higher in importance.
2. The goals in work with the individual child were centered on attempts to help him control or express his feelings appropriately, understand his relationships to others, or gain insight into his emotional problems.
3. The problems of the child in school were viewed as arising mostly from his personal characteristics, or those of his parents, and their family functioning. In turn, little recognition was given to the impact of school conditions upon a pupil or the total set of circumstances within the school which might be related to his poor adjustment.
4. A principal technique in work with the child was the interview, and its intent was to determine his feelings about and reactions to his home, his school, and his problems.
5. The chief emphasis was on helping the individual child accommodate himself to the school situation rather than on attempting to modify patterns within a school's operations which might be generating difficulties for him and for large numbers of other children as well.

Table B.1
Rank Order of Factor Means

Factor	Number of Tasks	Factor Mean*	Standard Deviation
2. Casework service to the child and his parents..........	13	2.90	.356
5. Caseload management...........	7	2.73	.549
6. Interpreting school social work service.............	8	2.72	.549
9. Clinical treatment of children with emotional problems..	6	2.71	.537
7. Liaison between the family and community agencies......	7	2.68	.541
8. Interpreting the child to the teacher.................	5	2.63	.591
3. Educational counseling with the child and his parents	12	2.31	.834
1. Leadership and policy-making..	18	2.20	.846

The means of factors differed significantly (that is, at the 5 percent level) with these exceptions: factors 5, 6, and 9; factors 6, 9, and 7; and factors 7 and 8 do not differ significantly.

6. Work with the child's parent was considered important mainly when it was necessary to clarify the child's problems or to obtain support for the social worker's activity in relation to the individual child.

7. Consultation with the teacher was defined principally in relation to an individual child and the social worker's service. Omitted from consultation with the teacher were areas of her work related to broader concerns, for example, use of peer relationships, use of group interaction in the classroom and on the playground, or assessment of children's functioning in relation to the general characteristics of the school in which they were pupils.

8. Activity with community agencies was defined in ways that supported the school social worker's efforts with an individual child—by giving or securing information in order to facilitate referrals or supporting and encouraging parents to use existing community services to which they had been referred.

By contrast with these highly rated tasks, school social workers rated as significantly less important those tasks that described work with children and their parents in relation to the child's educational goals, values, abilities, and interests and the social and academic expectations and regulations of the school (Factor 3). Least important of all were the tasks in Factor 1 which focused upon activities such as these: professional research; in-service training; publication of new findings and perspectives; recruitment of social work personnel; work with parents to help them understand and channel their concerns about the problems of their school system; improvement of working conditions of school staff; consultation with administrators on the formulation of pupil-welfare policy; and work in the community to bring about new social welfare services or social change.

When mean ratings for each factor were computed for seven geographical regions (states grouped for NASW regional institutes), school social workers showed a pattern of consistent agreement on the definition of school social work described above. The agreement was also apparent for social workers from school systems of varying size, except that social workers from the largest systems rated Factor 3, "Educational coun-seling with the child and his parents," significantly lower than did the social workers in each of the three smaller-size systems.

ASSIGNING SCHOOL SOCIAL WORK TASKS TO OTHER PERSONNEL

On the basis of the ratings from the question, "Can the task appropriately be assigned to a person with less than your level of education and professional preparation?" a mean rating was computed for each of the 107 items on the scale, as well as the overall mean for each group of items within a factor.

The overall factor means reflected a general prevalence of low ratings. Factor means ranged from a high of 1.54 for "Caseload management" to a low of .82 for "Clinical treatment of children with emotional problems." The range of responses for all 107 items was from a high of 2.18 to a low of 0.39. Only three tasks were rated higher than 2.0. These low ratings were in contrast to the ratings on importance of the tasks, which were generally high, suggesting that school social workers are inclined to see most of their activity as quite important and are reluctant to consider the delegation of very much of it. Even "Caseload management," which received the highest ratings on "assignability" ($m = 1.54$; s.d. $= 1.03$), reflected social workers' opinions that such tasks should be delegated less often than "frequently." It will be recalled that this factor contains fairly routine tasks, which probably can be rather easily delimited and directed. Similarly, tasks in "Educational counseling with the child and his family" ($m = 1.45$; s.d. $= 0.958$) and "Interpreting school social work service" ($m = 1.05$; s.d. $= 1.06$) were rated on the average as assignable "occasionally," but not "frequently."

Three factors had mean ratings so low as to indicate that social workers believe the task can never be assigned to persons with less than professional preparation. These factors—"Interpreting the child to the teacher" ($m = 0.92$; s.d. $= 0.931$), "Casework service to the child and his parents" ($m = 0.92$; s.d. $= 1.01$), and "Clinical treatment of children with emotional problems" ($m = 0.82$; s.d. $= 0.947$)—contain the core tasks of the definition of school social work described earlier, which gives priority to work with the individual child in relation to his personal and emotional problems and interpreting the child and his problems to the teacher.

For Factor 1, "Leadership and policy-making" ($m = 1.18$; s.d. $= 1.02$), a rank-order correlation between the mean ratings on task importance and the mean ratings on task assignability was -0.56 ($p < 0.05$); therefore, the more a task within this factor was considered to be important, the less willing social workers were to assign it to persons with less than their professional preparation. An inspection of the ratings shows that relatively high ratings were given to tasks that involve work with school administrators, interpreting the nature of school social work to community groups, publication of new findings about school social work, assisting with in-service training of teachers or administrators, or giving field instruction to graduate social work students. Relatively low ratings were given for tasks such as participation in social action groups in the community, working for new programs, participating in community planning councils, and working with groups of parents.

For Factor 7, "Liaison between the family and community agencies" ($m = 1.13$; s.d. $= 1.03$), a rank-order correlation of -0.78 ($10 > p > 0.05$) was found between ratings of importance and ratings of assignability. Relatively high importance ratings had been given to tasks involved in the process of referral to community agencies (for example, obtaining information from parents about family functioning to use in referral, or negotiating between agency and family until service gets under way), suggesting that the professional social worker sees these tasks as more appropriate for his own level of education, rather than "nonprofessional." Relatively low importance ratings were given to the obtaining of more routine kinds of information for use in referral, or encouraging the family, after referral is effected, to use the agency service. Apparently school social workers regard these tasks as "assignable."

None of the other factors showed any significant correlation between mean importance ratings and assignability ratings.

CONCLUSIONS

The general conclusions of the study may be summarized as follows:

1. The definition of school social work revealed by this study reflects the school social work literature of the 1940s and 1950s and shows little or no general response to the concerns expressed in both education and social work literature of the 1960s in relation to the learning problems of many unsuccessful schoolchildren and youth; the underlying conditions in the school, neighborhood, and community which contribute to their difficulties; and new approaches to use in the delivery of services to them.

2. The definition is a static one, which reflects a residual conception of social welfare. It largely ignores the most pressing problems of the school population, the underlying conditions which produce these problems, and the relationship of the school and its operations to those of other social institutions in the community.

3. The definition does not provide a promising basis for experimentation in assigning responsibility to social work staff with different levels of education. The definition commits its professional personnel to use up its resources in providing a limited range of social work services, without sufficient attention to the most pressing problems of schoolchildren and youth, problems which would lend themselves to experimentation in design of services and staffing patterns. School social workers seem unready to delegate many of the tasks that they regard as important, a finding that grows logically from the definition of school social work which they evolved.

DISCUSSION

Social workers in the schools serve in one of the most significant of the community's institutions, and they occupy a strategic position for exercising professional leadership within the school and its neighborhoods and community. However, the definition of school social work developed in this study does not support the readiness of school social workers to assume such responsibility and opportunity, evidenced by the relatively low level of importance accorded tasks of leadership and policy-making. For social workers to assign such a minor role to these tasks suggests that they deny how important it is for social work in every setting that the schools have sound curriculum and pupil-welfare policy and that children be enabled to make full use of improved educational resources. The fact that school social workers function in a secondary setting does not abrogate their responsibility for professional leadership. Social work in the schools is based on an interrelationship of problems and goals between the public school and the institution of social welfare; social work professional resources should not be used in another institution unless social workers have a share in the formulation of policy that affects the daily welfare and future opportunities and attainments of large numbers of children and youth.

The finding that social workers were reluctant to delegate the tasks that they considered important might be interpreted as indicating that generally they are not ready to look for solutions to the profession's crucial problem of manpower. However, it is unlikely that school social workers are simply unresponsive to the problem; undoubtedly they are also troubled by the shortage of qualified social work staff, the heavy work loads, and their inability to give full coverage in the services they provide. The observed reluctance to share school social work activity probably should be seen as a logical concomitant of the particular definition of school social work to which school social workers seem committed.

School social workers during the 1940s and 1950s put great professional energy into developing casework service in the public schools. That in doing so they gave up the earlier tasks of school-home-community liaison and of bringing about social change in the community is not unlike what can be documented in other areas of social work practice during these same years. As school social workers sought to refine their casework service, they developed conviction that their work required "a special competence and skill," and they accepted the traditional view that their forms of social work activity were properly reserved for the graduate social worker. In the face of growing shortages of professional workers and the resulting concern to protect the quality of service, the tendency of school social workers probably was to maintain a narrowed range of services—those which the profession had long seen as the province of the graduate social worker.

Because professional social workers in schools apparently have not responded sufficiently to the community's most pressing problems and to the experimentation and demonstrations of new kinds of service which have gone on in some schools in recent years, they are still in possession of a traditional model of social work service which has not required them to make a critical examination of their staffing pattern.

Any effective plan for differential recruitment and use of social work staff must be built around an identification of the core problems of the client group and a re-assessment of the goals of the social work service. As problems and conditions of the school and schoolchildren are restudied, the goals of the social work service then can be re-assessed, and if these goals are defined in response to the most pressing problems of schoolchildren and their families, then the purpose of the school in the community can be seen to serve not as a therapeutic center but as a life setting for children and youth where learning is possible and competence can be acquired. School social services then become preventive services as they help to make school a place in which more children and youth can learn, an environment for acquiring the skills for today's job market, for progression into higher education, and for developing an image of one's self as a person who is capable, who can learn and succeed. Effects such as these are truly preventive of future problems.

With goals that meet these terms, social work can move anew toward the school in a spirit of partnership to establish a contract for service. That is, the social worker can approach the school administrator and other school personnel in ways that do not invite or exacerbate defensiveness about "crisis in the school" but that lead to the development and achievement of a sense of common purpose and that set forth that "this is what we think we can do in relation to these problems and this is what you can expect of us."

To meet new goals, changes in services must be considered. The following are examples:

1. Early and continued consultation with school administrators is necessary in order to examine the symptoms and determine the causes of pupil problems in a school system, to channel back knowledge about neighborhood and community influences in the lives of the pupils, to encourage administrators to develop cooperative working relationships with community agencies, and to consult in the formulation of administrative policy that directly affects the welfare of pupils.

2. Consultation with teachers should continue as an important part of school social work, but with a broader focus—one that will include interpretation of social forces in an effort to modify teachers' perceptions of children with limited backgrounds and to help them mold a climate in which children are freed and motivated to learn.

3. Different points for social work intervention in a pupil's difficulty must be considered, and new strategies for change must be tried out.

4. There must be a broader application of the group work method in the school setting. The group approach to schoolchildren with problems, or potential problems, is reported increasingly in the social work literature and in conference discussions. Its usefulness has long been acknowledged, and its fuller application is overdue.

5. There is increasing attention to the rights of parents in relation to the school their children attend and recognition of the importance of parents' involvement in school affairs. Social workers should find ways of working with parents to help them constructively channel their concern about their school system to the proper school authorities.

6. In addition to trying to effect a stronger liaison with existing community agencies for service to schoolchildren and their families, school social workers must find ways to assist with planned change in the organizational pattern of social welfare programs and resources, or to act as catalysts to those agents in the community whose primary function is to change the pattern of the social structure of our society.

Broadening the base of school social workers' ability to respond to today's pressing problems in the community and in the school cannot come about solely through in-service training and some workers' readiness to experiment. Social work education must respond more fully and quickly to the interests of students in working with the community and its social institutions; it must educate for new functions, and teach not only all social work methods but alternative approaches within these methods. School social workers cannot employ techniques that they have not learned; nor can they consult with teachers, school administrators, and community leaders about problems of which they have no understanding.

Moreover, we cannot expect a program of in-service training to compensate fully for the fact that most bachelor's degree social workers have not had planned undergraduate education in the field of social welfare. Greater progress in undergraduate social work education is needed.

The conclusions and implications for practice and education which have been drawn from this study's findings are not intended to detract from the richness in the course of development of school social work or from the accomplishments of numerous school social workers who have worked with diligence and conviction to help children in their school life. Changing times and new problems always bring need for evaluation of well-established patterns of work. School social workers want no less as they continue their efforts to find effective ways of helping troubled children and youth.

Received October 17, 1968

APPENDIX [to Appendix B]:
DESCRIPTION OF THE FACTORS

Items loading at 0.40 or over made up the following factors:

1. Leadership and policy-making

Assists in in-service training of teachers or administrators; participates in research projects; publishes new finding and perspectives on social work services in the school setting; assists in the recruiting of social work personnel; assists in the education of social work personnel (for example, field instruction of graduate social work students); works actively to obtain increased salaries and improved working conditions for teachers and other school personnel; consults with school administrators in the formulation of administrative policy which directly affects the welfare of pupils; works with school administrators, individually or in groups, to examine the symptoms and determine causes of problems in the school system; encourages administrators to develop cooperative working relationships with community agencies; helps to bring about new outside-of-school programs through work with other individuals and community groups; accepts responsibilities within a community council or other planning and coordinating group; attends and contributes to meetings of social action groups, aside from professional social work or education organizations; interprets the nature of social work services to other community agencies or interest groups through speeches, panel discussions, and so on; helps interpret to the community the school administrative policies which have to do with pupil welfare; plans or conducts educational meetings with groups of parents to increase their knowledge about their children's development, their role as parents, and so on; works with groups of parents to organize and channel their concerns about the problems of their school system; participates in staffings, even when the child is not known to the social worker, in order to remain familiar with as many children in the building as possible; does informal long-range follow-up on completed cases by talking to teacher, friends, parents, or child.

2. Casework service to the child and his parents

Obtains psychiatric, psychological, or social casework consultations when problems in diagnosis occur; obtains from parents information on the child's behavior at home and his previous development and experiences; consults with other special service personnel to develop and coordinate an overall treatment approach for the child; selects and periodically revises the plan for service and its goals; obtains from various school personnel a description of the child's problems and his behavior at school, both in and out of the classroom; involves the principal in plans concerning a case and suggests ways he may help deal with the problem; helps the child control or express his feelings appropriately; helps the child develop new attitudes or modify old ones; helps the child understand his relationships to important adults in his life; clarifies with the parents the nature of the child's problems; helps parents see how they contribute to their child's growth (that is, recognize their own particular strengths as parents); helps parents see how they contribute to their child's problems (for example, through their own marital problems, poor home conditions, or by their particular methods of child care); helps parents develop realistic perceptions of their child's academic potential and performance, his limitations, and his future.

3. *Educational counseling with the child and his parents*

Interprets to the child the nature of the school's authority over him; interprets to the child the nature of his parents' authority over him; clarifies the school's social and academic expectations and regulations with the child; offers factual information; helps the child develop his educational goals or values; offers advice, suggestions, and direction; helps the child understand his abilities and interests; interprets to the child reasons for his behavior and his relationship to others; interprets to parents who are ignoring school regulations the nature of the school's authority and its expectations; clarifies with the parents the school's social and academic expectations and regulations; makes suggestions as to how the parents can improve their relations with their child's teacher and with his school; checks on attendance by making home visits in cases of prolonged or unexplained absences.

4. *Personal service to teacher*

Refers the teacher to a community agency for help with personal problems when the teacher's own difficulties prevent her from being effective in her work; helps the teacher understand her own personal problems; refers the teacher to a community agency for help with her own personal problems, even though they are not interfering with her work; acquaints teacher with and encourages her to use community services, especially those available for her direct use with the child and his family; discusses with the teacher the nature of her interactions with the child; helps teacher plan how she will interpret to the child the referral for service and the role of the social worker.

5. *Caseload management*

Sets up appointments with child, parents, or other appropriate persons; channels information, such as referrals, suggestions, and releases, to appropriate personnel; reviews the child's cumulative record and takes notes on pertinent information; supplies information to parents about welfare agencies or public health facilities (for example, location, application procedures, and so on); helps teacher discover the child's resources for achieving success; maintains required records of social work service, keeps schedule of activities up to date, and writes reports of services; explains the ways in which a child's emotional or social problems may affect his academic performance.

6. *Interpreting school social work service*

Describes to other special service personnel the range of services the social worker is able to provide; describes to the teacher the nature, objectives and procedures of school social work service; explains to the child why he has been referred for social work service; makes regular visits to parents to maintain a liaison between home and school to reinforce parents' interest and concern for their child's school life; participates on school committees to improve effectiveness of all the special services; clears referrals with teacher and principal when the referral has originated elsewhere; explains to the child how they will work together (for example, time and place of appointments; the worker's contact with his teacher and parents).

7. *Liaison between the family and community agencies*

Obtains from parents information about the family's functioning; actively encourages child or family to make maximum use of community resources to which they have been referred, and gives continuing positive support to them in their attempts; assesses the child's functioning in relation to his neighborhood patterns and other cultural influences; acts as a liaison between a family and social agency to insure that, following referral, service gets under way; obtains information from other agencies that have had experience with the child and/or his family; obtains information about the child's medical problems from the family physician; encourages children and families to ask for and make maximum use of community "supplementary" or "enabling" services.

8. *Interpreting the child to the teacher*

Assesses the improvement which can be expected in the child and/or family; discusses whether the problem is suitable for service; offers suggestions concerning how to deal with parents; distinguishes between normal and problem behavior in a child; helps the teacher recognize possible differences in the values of the child and teacher.

9. *Clinical treatment of children with emotional problems*

Helps the child gain insight into his emotional problems; helps the child develop his personal goals or values; helps the child change his overt behavior in life situations; works with an individual child in a casework relationship; works with groups of children, using the group process; interviews child to determine his feelings and reactions concerning his home, his school, and his problems.

NOTES

1. Program and services were furnished by the Research Section of the Statistical Services Unit of the University of Illinois.

2. For a full and technical description of the method used see Harmon (2).

3. A table for each factor, showing the variance accounted for by items in that factor, the items which loaded .40 or above, and the mean and standard deviation of responses to each item is included in Appendix B of the report (5).

REFERENCES

1. Coleman, James S., et al. *Equality of Educational Opportunity*. Washington, D.C.: U.S. Government Printing Office, 1966.
2. Harmon, Harry H. *Modern Factor Analysis*. 2d rev. ed. Chicago: University of Chicago Press, 1967.
3. Schafer, Walter E., and Kenneth Polk. "Delinquency and the Schools." In *Task Force Report: Juvenile Delinquency and Youth Crime. Report on Juvenile Justice and Consultants' Papers*, by the Task Force on Juvenile Delinquency, President's Commission on Law Enforcement and Administration of Justice. Washington, D.C.: U.S. Government Printing Office, 1967.
4. U.S. Department of Health, Education, and Welfare. *Closing the Gap in Social Work Manpower: Report of the Departmental Task Force on Social Work and Education and Manpower*. Washington, D.C.: U.S. Government Printing Office, 1965.
5. ———. Office of Education. Bureau of Research. "An Analysis of School Social Work as a Basis for Improved Use of Staff." Final Report on Project No. 6-8315, Grant No. OEG 3-6-068315-1306. February 28, 1968.
6. Witte, Ernest F. "The Current Situation and Foreseeable Trends in Social Work Education." In *Manpower: A Community Responsibility*. Arden House Workshop, August 13–16, 1967. New York: National Association of Social Workers, 1968.

References

Abbott, E., and S. Breckinridge. 1917. *Truancy and Non-Attendance in the Chicago Schools*. Chicago: University of Chicago Press.

Abbott, M. C. 1965. Hierarchial impediments to innovation in educational organizations. In M. C. Abbott and T. J. Lowell, eds., *Change Perspectives in Education Administration*. Auburn, Ala.: Auburn University.

Alderson, J. 1969. *Social Work in Schools: Patterns and Perspectives*. Northbrok, Ill.: Whitehall.

————. 1972. Models of school social work practice. In R. Sarri and F. Maple, eds., *The School in the Community*. Washington, D.C.: NASW.

Alderson, J. J., and C. H. Krisef. 1973. Another perspective on tasks in school social work. *Social Casework*, 54: 591–600.

Alkin, M. C., R. Daillak, and P. White. 1979. *Using Evaluations: Does Evaluation Make a Difference?* Beverly Hills: Sage.

Allen-Meares, P., R. O. Washington, and B. L. Welsh. 1986. *Social Work Services in the Schools*. Englewood Cliffs, N.J.: Prentice Hall.

Altmeyer, J. R. 1956. Public school services for children with emotional problems. *Social Work*, 1: 96–102.

Anderson, R. 1975. Introducing change in school–community–pupil relationships: Maintaining credibility and accountability. *Journal of Education for Social Work*, 10: 3–8.

Areson, C. W. 1933. Status of children's work in the United States. *Proceedings of the National Conference of Social Work*. Chicago: University of Chicago Press.

Argyris, C. 1957. *Personality and Organization*. New York: Harper Brothers.

Baldridge, J. V. 1975. Organizational innovation: Individual, structural,and environmental impacts. In J. V. Baldridge and T. E. Deal, eds., *Managing Change in Educational Organizations*. Berkeley: McCutchan.

Barnard, C. 1946. Functions and pathology of status systems in formal organizations. In W. F. Whyte, ed., *Industry and Society*. New York: McGraw-Hill.

Beck, B. 1958. The adolescent challenge to casework. *Social Work*, 3: 89–95.

Ben-David, J. 1962. Scientific productivity and academic organization in nineteenth-century medicine. In B. Barber and W. Hirsch, eds., *The Sociology of Science.* New York: Free Press.

Bennis, W. G. 1971. Changing organizations. In H. A. Hornstein, B. B. Burker, W. W. Burke, M. Gindis, and R. J. Lewicki, eds., *Social Intervention: A Behavioral Science Approach.* New York: Free Press.

Bennis, W. G., K. D. Benne, and R. Chin, eds. 1962. *The Planning of Change.* New York: Holt, Rinehart, & Winston.

Bernard, L. L., and J. Bernard. 1943. *Origins of American Sociology.* New York: Crowell.

Beyer, J. M., and H. M. Trice. 1982. The utilization process: A conceptual framework and synthesis of empirical findings. *Administration Science Quarterly,* 27: 591–622.

Blau, P. M. 1955. *Bureaucracy in Modern Society.* New York: Random House.

Blau, P. M., and R. Scott. 1962. *Formal Organizations.* San Francisco: Chandler.

Bradburn, N. M., and S. Sudman. 1980. *Improving Interview Methods and Questionnaire Design.* San Francisco: Jossey-Bass.

Breckinridge, S. B. 1914. Some aspects of the public school from a school social worker's point of view. *Proceedings of the National Education Association.* Ann Arbor, Mich.: National Education Association.

Bremner, R. J., ed. 1971. *Children and Youth in America: A Documentary History.* 3 vols. Cambridge, Mass.: Harvard University Press.

Briar, S., H. Weissman, and A. Rubin. 1981. *Research Utilization in Social Work.* New York: Council on Social Work Education.

Brown, J. A. 1982. The school as an organization: An approach to problem solving in the school setting. In R. T. Constable and J. Flynn, eds., *School Social Work: Practice and Research Perspectives.* Homewood, Ill.: Dorsey Press.

Brown, R. D., L. A., Braskamp, and D. L. Newman. 1978. Evaluator credibility as a function of report style—Do jargon and data make a difference? *Evaluation Quarterly,* 2: 331–41.

Burns, T., and G. M. Stalker. 1961. *The Management of Innovation.* London: Tavistock.

Caplan, N. 1976. Factors associated with knowledge use among federal executives. *Policy Studies Journal,* 4: 229–34.

Caplan, N. A., A. Morrison, and R. J. Stambaugh. 1975. *The Use of Social Science Knowledge in Policy Decisions at the National Level.* Ann Arbor, Mich.: Institute for Social Research.

Carr, L. 1976. National Association of Social Workers Report on survey of social work services in schools. Mimeographed.

Chavkin, N. F. 1985. School social work practice: A reappraisal. *Social Work in Education,* 8: 3–13.

———. 1986. The practice-research relationship: An organizational link. *Social Service Review,* 60: 241–50.

———. 1989. Linking schools and parents. *Social Work in Education,* 11: 149–59.

———. 1990. Multicultural approaches to parent involvement: Research and practice. *Social Work in Education,* 13: 22–33.

———. 1991. Uniting families and schools: Social workers helping teachers through inservice training. *School Social Work Journal,* 15: 1–10.

Chavkin, N. F., and K. Brown. 1992. School social workers build a multi-ethnic family-school-community partnership. *Social Work in Education,* 14: 160–164.

Chavkin, N. F., and M. Garza-Lubeck. 1988. The role of parent involvement in recruiting and retaining the Hispanic college student. *College and University*, 63: 310–22.

Cherns, A. B. 1970. Relations between research institutions and users of research. *International Social Science Journal*, 22: 226–42.

Cillie, F. 1940. *Centralization or Decentralization: A Study in Educational Adaptation.* New York: Teachers College, Columbia University.

Coleman, J. V. 1951. Meeting the mental health needs of children in school today: Psychiatric implications for the practice of school social work. *Bulletin of the National Association of School Social Workers*, 27: 3–13. Reprinted in G. Lee, ed., *Helping the Troubled School Child.* New York: NASW, 1959.

Conner, R. F. 1981. Measuring evaluation utilization: A critique of different techniques. In J. A. Ciarlo, ed., *Utilizing Evaluation: Concepts and Measurement Techniques.* Beverly Hills: Sage.

Constable, R. 1979. Toward the construction of role in an emergent social work specialization. *School Social Work Quarterly*, 1: 135–48.

Constable, R. T., and J. P. Flynn, eds. 1979. *School Social Work: Practice and Research Perspectives.* Homewood, Ill.: Dorsey Press.

Cook, T. D. 1978. Introduction. In T. D. Cook et al., eds., *Evaluation Studies Review Annual.* Beverly Hills: Sage.

Corwin, R. G. 1972. Strategies for organizational innovation: An empirical comparison. *American Sociological Review*, 37: 441–54.

Costin, L. B. 1969a. An analysis of the tasks in school social work. *Social Service Review*, 43: 274–85.

———. 1969b. A historical review of school social work. *Social Casework*, 50: 439–53.

———. 1972. Adaptations in the delivery of school social work services. *Social Casework*, 53: 348–54.

———. 1975. School social work practice: A new model. *Social Work*, 20: 135–39.

———. 1978. *Social Work Services in Schools: Historical Perspectives and Current Directions.* Washington, D.C.: NASW.

Cremin, L. A. 1961. *The Transformation of the School.* New York: Alfred A. Knopf.

Culbert, J. 1929. *The Visiting Teacher at Work.* New York: The Commonwealth Fund and the Public Education Association of the City of New York.

Daft, R. L., and S. W. Becker. 1978. *Innovation in Organizations.* New York: Elsevier.

Dery, D. 1986. Knowledge and organizations. *Policy Studies Review*, 6: 14–25.

Dewey, J. 1902. *The Child and the Curriculum.* Chicago: University of Chicago Press.

Ellis, M. B. 1925. *The Visiting Teacher in Rochester.* New York: Joint Committee on Methods of Preventing Delinquency.

Etzioni, A. 1964. *Modern Organizations.* Englewood Cliffs, N.J.: Prentice Hall.

Everett, E. M. 1931. The importance of social work in a school program. *The Family*, 19: 308. Reprinted in G. Lee, ed., *Helping the Troubled School Child.* New York: NASW, 1959.

Fisher, J. K. 1966. Role perceptions and characteristics of attendance coordinators, psychologists, and social workers. *Journal of International Association of Pupil Personnel Workers*, 10: 1–8.

Follett, M. P. 1924. *Creative Experience.* New York: Longmans, Green.

Flynn, J. P. 1976. Congruence in perception of social work-related tasks in a school system. *Social Service Review*, 50: 471–81.

Franklin, C., and C. L. Streeter. 1991. Evidence for the effectiveness of social work with high school dropout youths. *Social Work in Education*, 13: 307–27.

Freeman, E. M., and M. Pennekamp. 1988. *Social Work Practice: Toward a Child, Family, School, Community Perspective*. Springfield, Ill.: Charles C. Thomas.

Getzels, J. W., and E. G. Guba. 1957. Social behavior and the administrative process. *School Review*, 65: 423–41.

Glaser, E. M., ed. 1976. *Putting Knowledge to Use: A Distillation of the Literature Regarding Knowledge Transfer and Change*. Beverly Hills: Human Interaction Research Institute.

Gouldner, A. W. 1959. Organizational analysis. In R. K. Merton, L. Broom, and L. S. Cottrell, Jr., eds., *Sociology Today*. New York: Basic Books.

Grasso, A. J., and I. Epstein, eds. 1992. *Research Utilization in the Social Services: Innovations for Practice and Administration*. New York: The Haworth Press.

Griffiths, D. E. 1964. Administrative theory and change in organizations. In M. B. Miles, ed., *Innovation in Education*. New York: Teachers College, Columbia University.

Gross, N., J. B. Giacquinta, and M. Bernstein. 1971. *Implementing Organizational Innovations: A Sociological Analysis of Planned Educational Change*. New York: Basic Books.

Gulick, L., and L. Urwick, eds. 1937. *Papers on the Science of Administration*. New York: Institute of Public Administration.

Guzzetta, C. 1972. School social work leadership. In M. J. Austin et al., eds., *Continuing Education in Social Welfare: School Social Work and the Effective Use of Manpower*. Tallahassee: State University of Florida.

Hage, J. 1965. An axiomatic theory of organizations. *Administrative Science Quarterly*, 10: 289–321.

Hage, J., and M. Aiken. 1967. Program change and organizational properties: A comparative analysis. *American Journal of Sociology*, 72: 503–19.

———. 1970. *Social Change in Complex Organizations*. New York: Random House,

Hall, R. 1963. The concept of bureaucracy: An empirical assessment. *American Journal of Sociology*, 69: 32–40.

———. 1972. *Organizations, Structure and Process*. Englewood Cliffs, N.J.: Prentice Hall.

Hasenfeld, Y., and R. English. 1974. *Human Service Organizations*. Ann Arbor, Mich.: University of Michigan Press.

Hasenfeld, Y., and R. Patti. 1992. The utilization of research in administrative practice. In A. J. Grasso and I. Epstein, eds., *Research Utilization in the Social Services*. New York: Haworth Press.

Havelock, R. G. 1971. *Planning for Innovation Through Dissemination and Utilization of Knowledge*, 2d ed. Ann Arbor, Mich.: Institute for Social Research, University of Michigan.

Hawkins, M. T. 1979. State Standards for Certificated School Social Worker, Visiting Teacher, Attendance Worker, and Home-School Visitor. Unpublished Ph.D. dissertation, University of Pittsburgh.

Holt, J. 1964. *How Children Fail*. New York: Pitman.

———. 1967. *How Children Learn*. New York: Pitman.

Holzner, B. 1978. The sociology of applied knowledge. *Sociological Symposium*, 21: 8–9.

Holzner, B., and J. H. Marx. 1979. *Knowledge Application: The Knowledge System in Society.* Boston: Allyn & Bacon.

Jackson, J. M. 1959. The organization and its communication problem. *Journal of Communication,* 9: 158–72.

Johnson, A. 1962. *School Social Work: Its Contribution to Professional Education.* New York: NASW.

Johnson, P. A. 1978. The Relationship of Centralization with Other Characteristics of Formal Organizations and Selected Environmental Variables. Unpublished Ph.D. dissertation, University of Texas, Austin.

Kahn, A. 1972. The school: Social change and social welfare. In R. C. Sarri and F. F. Maple, eds., *The School in the Community.* Washington, D.C.: NASW, 1972.

Katz, D., and R. L. Kahn. 1966. *The Social Psychology of Organizations.* New York: John Wiley.

Kennedy, P. A., and N. F. Chavkin. 1992. Access to higher education for all. *Educational Leadership,* 62: 24–27.

Knorr, K. D. 1977. Policymakers' use of social science knowledge: Symbolic or instrumental? In C. H. Weiss, ed., *Using Social Science Research in Public Policy Making.* Lexington, Mass.: D. C. Heath.

Kogan, L. S. 1963. The utilization of social work research. *Social Casework,* 34: 569–74.

Kohl, H. R. 1970. *The Open Classroom.* New York: Vintage Books.

Kozol, J. 1967. *Death at an Early Age.* Boston: Houghton Mifflin.

Labovitz, S. 1970. The assignment of numbers to rank order categories. *American Sociological Review,* 35: 515–24.

———. 1972. Statistical usage in sociology. *Sociological Methods & Research,* 1: 13–37.

Lambert, C., and R. Mullaly. 1982. School social work: The congruence of task importance and level of effort. In R. T. Constable and J. P. Flynn, eds., *School Social Work: Practice and Research Perspectives.* Homewood, Ill.: Dorsey Press.

Lawrence, P. R., and J. W. Lorsch. 1967. Differentiation and integration in complex organizations. *Administrative Science Quarterly,* 12: 1–47.

Lazarsfeld, P. F., and J. G. Reitz. 1975. *An Introduction to Applied Sociology.* New York: Elsevier.

Lazarsfeld, P. F., Sewell, W. H. and H. L. Wilensky, eds. 1967. *The Uses of Sociology.* New York: Basic Books.

LeCroy, C. W., J. B. Ashford, and M. W. Macht. 1989. A framework for analyzing knowledge utilization in social work practice. *Journal of Sociology and Social Welfare,* 16: 3–17.

Lee, G. ed. 1959. *Helping the Troubled School Child.* New York: NASW.

Leedy, P. D. 1980. *Practical Research: Planning and Design.* New York: Macmillan.

Leiby, J. 1978. *A History of Social Welfare and Social Work in the United States.* New York: Columbia University Press.

Levine, R. S., P. Allen-Meares, and F. Easton. 1987. Primary prevention and the educational preparation of school social workers. *Social Work in Education,* 9: 145–58.

Levitan, L. C., and E. F. X. Hughes. 1981. Research on the utilization of evaluations: A review and synthesis. *Evaluation Review,* 5: 525–48.

Lide, P. 1953. A study of the historical influences of major importance in determining the present functioning of the school social worker. *Bulletin of NASSW*, 29: 18–32. Reprinted in G. Lee, ed., *Helping the Troubled School Child*. Newark: NASW, 1959.

Likert, R. 1961. *New Patterns of Management*. New York: McGraw-Hill.

Litchfield, E. H. 1956. Notes on a general theory of administration. *Administrative Science Quarterly*, 1: 3–29.

Lubove, R. 1973. *The Professional Altruist: The Emergence of Social Work as a Career (1880–1930)*. New York: Atheneum.

Lynn, L. E. 1978. *Knowledge and Policy: The Uncertain Connection*. Washington, D.C.: National Academy of Sciences.

Mattaini, M. A. 1992. Research and practice: Bridging the gap: Introduction to the special issue. *Research on Social Work Practice*, 2: 261–62.

Mayer, R. R., and E. Greenwood. 1980. *The Design of Social Policy Research*. Englewood Cliffs, N.J.: Prentice Hall.

McGregor, D. 1960. *The Human Side of Enterprise*. New York: McGraw-Hill.

Meares, P. 1977. Analysis of tasks in school social work. *Social Work*, 22: 196–201.

Merton, R. K. 1949. The role of applied social science in the formation of policy: A research memorandum. *Philosophy of Science*, 16: 161–81.

―――. 1960. Bureaucratic structure and personality. In A. Etzioni, ed., *Complex Organizations: A Sociological Reader*. New York: Holt, Rinehart, and Winston.

Miles, M. G., ed. 1964. *Innovation in Education*. New York: Teachers College, Columbia University.

Mitchell, G. W. 1957. Casework with the school child. *Social Work*, 2: 77–83.

Mizrahi, T. 1992. The future of research utilization in community practice. In A. J. Grasso and I. Epstein, eds., *Research Utilization in the Social Services*. New York: Haworth Press.

Mullen, E. J. 1978. The construction of personal models for effective practice: A method for utilizing research findings to guide social interventions. *Journal of Social Service Research*, 2: 45–63.

National Academy of Science. 1978. *The Federal Investment in Knowledge of Social Problems*. Washington, D.C.: National Academy of Sciences.

National Association of Social Workers. 1956. *Curriculum Content Specific to and Deriving from the Field of Social Work*. New York: NASW.

National Institute of Mental Health. 1991. *Caring for People with Severe Mental Disorders: A National Plan of Research to Improve Services*. DHHS Publication No. ADM 91-1762. Washington, D.C.: Government Printing Office.

Nudd, H. W. 1927. The school and social work. *Proceedings of National Conference of Social Work*. Chicago: University of Chicago Press.

Nystrom, J. F. 1989. Empowerment model for delivery of social work services in public schools. *Social Work in Education*, 11: 160–70.

Oberschall, A. 1973. *The Establishment of Empirical Sociology: Studies in Continuity, Discontinuity, and Institutionalism*. New York: Harper and Row.

Oppenheimer, J. J. 1924. *The Visiting Teacher Movement with Special Reference to Administrative Relationships*. New York: Public Education Association.

Parr, G., and H. Alstein. 1979. Social work in a Catholic school system. *Social Work in Education*, 4: 5–21.

Patton, M. Q. 1979. *Utilization Focused Evaluation*. Beverly Hills: Sage Publications.

Patton, M. Q., P. S. Grimes, K. N. Guthrie, N. J. Brennan, A, French, and D. Blyth.

1977. In search of impact: An analysis of the utilization of federal health evaluation research. In C. H. Weiss, ed., *Using Social Research in Public Policy Making*. Lexington, Mass.: Lexington Books.

Pelz, D. G., and F. M. Andrews. 1966. *Scientists in Organizations: Productive Climates for Research and Development*. New York: John Wiley.

Perrow, C. 1967. A framework for the comparative analysis of organizations. *American Sociological Review*, 32: 192–208.

Pins, A. M. 1966. *Contemporary Education for Social Work in the United States*. New York: CSWE.

Reeves, J. 1978. Influence of Organizational Characteristics and Environmental Factors on Job Satisfaction and Adaptiveness in School Districts. Unpublished Ph.D. dissertation, University of Texas, Austin.

Reid, W. J. 1993. Toward a research-oriented profession: An essay review of Task Force on Social Work Research, *Building Social Work Knowledge for Effective Services and Policies—A Plan for Research Development. Research on Social Work Practice*, 3: 103–13.

Rein, M. 1976. *Social Science and Public Policy*. New York: Penguin.

Report of the National Advisory Committee on Civil Disorders. 1968. Washington, D.C.: U.S. Government Printing Office.

Rich, R. F. 1977. Use of social science information by federal bureaucrats: Knowledge for action versus knowledge for understanding. In C. H. Weiss, ed., *Using Social Research in Public Policy Making*. Lexington, Mass.: Lexington Books.

———. 1981. Problem-solving and evaluation research: Unemployed insurance policy. In J. F. Ciarlo, ed., *Utilizing Evaluation: Concepts and Measurement Techniques*. Beverly Hills: Sage.

Richmond, M. 1917. *Social Diagnosis*. New York: Russell Sage Foundation.

Rodney, H., and P. Kolodney. 1964. Organizational strains in the researcher practitioner relationship. *Human Organization*, 23: 171–82.

Rogers, E. M. 1962. *Diffusion of Innovations*. New York: Free Press.

Rosenblatt, A. 1968. The practitioner's use and evaluation of research. *Social Work*, 13: 53–59.

Ross, D., ed. 1958. *Administration for Adaptability*. New York: Metropolitan School Study Council.

Rothman, J. 1980. *Social R&D: Research and Development in the Human Services*. Englewood Cliffs, N.J.: Prentice-Hall.

Rowen, R. D. 1965. The function of the visiting teacher in the school. *Journal of International Association of Pupil Personnel Workers*, 9: 3–9.

Sarri, R., and F. Maple. 1972. *The School in the Community*. Washington, D.C.: NASW.

Schein, E. H. 1965. *Organizational Psychology*. Englewood Cliffs, N.J.: Prentice-Hall.

Schour, E. 1958. Casework with parents in the school setting. *Social Work*, 3: 68–75.

Shepard, H. A. 1967. Innovation-resisting and innovation-producing organizations. *Journal of Business*, 40: 470–77.

Sikkema, M. 1953. *Report of a Study of School Social Work Practice in Twelve Communities*. New York: American Association of Social Workers.

Silberman, C. E. 1970. *Crisis in the Classroom*. New York: Random House.

Simon, H. A. 1976. *Administrative Behavior*. New York: Free Press.

Snead, W. E. 1967. A Test of an Axiomatic Theory of Organizations in the Junior College Milieu. Unpublished Ph.D. dissertation, University of Texas, Austin.

Steiner, J. 1979. Social workers in school politics. *Social Work in Education*, 2: 41–57.

Tannenbaum, A. S. 1968. *Control in Organizations*. New York: McGraw-Hill.

Task Force on Social Work Research. 1991. *Building Social Work Knowledge for Effective Services and Policies: A Plan for Research Development*. Austin.

Taylor, F. 1911. *Scientific Management*. New York: Harper Brothers.

Thacker, L. C. 1978. Adaptiveness of School Districts as Related to Organizational Structure and Environmental Characteristics. Unpublished Ph.D. dissertation, University of Texas, Austin.

Thompson, J. D. 1967. *Organizations in Action*. New York: McGraw-Hill.

Thompson, P. A., R. D. Brown, and J. Furgason. 1981. Jargon and data do make a difference: The impact of report styles on lay and professional evaluation audiences. *Evaluation Review*, 5: 269–75.

Thompson, V. 1965. Bureaucracy and innovation. *Administrative Science Quarterly*, 10: 1–20.

Timberlake, E. M., C. A. Sabatino, and S. N. Hooper. 1982. School social work practice and P. L. 94–142. In R. T. Constable and J. P. Flynn, eds., *School Social Work: Practice and Research Perspectives*. Homewood, Ill.: Dorsey Press.

Tripodi, T., P. Fellin, and H. J. Meyer. 1969. *The Assessment of Social Research*. Itasca, Ill.: F. E. Peacock.

Videka-Sherman, L. 1986. *Studies of Research on Social Work Practice*. Silver Spring, Md.: National Association of Social Workers.

Vinter, R. 1963. Analysis of treatment organizations. *Social Work*, 8: 3–15.

Vinter, R. D., and R. C. Sarri. 1965. Malperformance in the public school: A group work approach. *Social Work*, 10: 3–13.

Walker, D. R. 1958. Use of the knowledge of the casework process in collaboration with school personnel. *Social Work*, 3: 97–103.

Watson, G., ed. 1967a. *Change in School Systems*. Washington, D.C.: NTL Institute for Applied Behavioral Science.

———. 1967b. *Concepts for Social Change*. Washington, D.C.: NTL Institute for Applied Behavioral Science.

Weatherly, R. 1978. Educating for survival in the school bureaucracy. *Social Work in Education*, 1: 19–28.

Weber, M. 1947. *The Theory of Social and Economic Organizations*, A. M. Henderson and T. Parsons, trans., and T. Parsons, ed. New York: Free Press.

Weiss, C. H., ed. 1972. *Evaluating Action Programs*. Boston: Allyn & Bacon.

———. 1977. *Using Social Research in Public Policy Making*. Lexington, Mass.: Lexington Books.

Weiss, C. H. 1981. Use of social science research in organizations: The constrained repertoire theory. In H. D. Stein, ed., *Organizations and the Human Services: Cross-Disciplinary Reflections*. Philadelphia: Temple University Press.

Weiss, C. H., and M. J. Bucuvalas. 1980. *Social Science Research and Decision-Making*. New York: Columbia University Press.

Weissman, H. 1992. Research utilization in administration and community practice. In A. J. Grasso and I. Epstein, eds. *Research Utilization in the Social Services*. New York: Haworth Press.

Williams, R. B. 1970. School compatibility and social work role. *Social Service Review*, 44: 169–76.

Williams, S. R., and J. A. Wysong. 1977. Health services research and health policy formulation: An empirical analysis and a structural solution. *Journal of Health Politics, Policy and Law*, 2:362–87.

Wilson, J. Q. 1966. Innovation in organization: Notes toward a theory. In J. D. Thompson, ed., *Approaches to Organizational Design*. Pittsburgh: University of Pittsburgh Press.

Winters, W. G., and F. Easton. 1983. *The Practice of Social Work in Schools: An Ecological Perspective*. New York: Free Press.

Woods, R. A., and A. J. Kennedy. 1922. *The Settlement Horizon*. New York: Russell Sage Foundation.

Wren, D. A. 1972. *The Evolution of Management Thought*. New York: Ronald Press.

Young, P. 1946. *Scientific Social Surveys and Research*. Englewood Cliffs, N.J.: Prentice Hall.

Zald, M. N., ed. 1967. *Organizing for Community Welfare*. Chicago: Quadrangle.

Zaltman, G., and R. Duncan. 1977. *Strategies for Planned Change*. New York: John Wiley.

Zaltman, G., R. Duncan, and J. Holbek. 1973. *Innovations and Organizations*. New York: John Wiley.

Zimbalist, S. E. 1977. *Historic Themes and Landmarks in Social Welfare Research*. New York: Harper & Row.

Zurcher, L. A., Jr., and C. M. Bonjean. 1970. *Planned Social Intervention*. Scranton, Pa.: Chandler.

Index

About the Author

NANCY FEYL CHAVKIN is an Associate Professor at the Richter Institute of Social Work at Southwest Texas State University. She is the author of more than thirty articles on research, parent involvement, school social work, and school-community partnerships. Her book *Families and Schools in a Pluralistic Society* was published in 1993.

Augsburg College
George Sverdrup Library
Minneapolis, MN 55454